THE JOY OF PRAYER

The Joy of Prayer

Copyright © 2023 Mark Morozov
Unless otherwise noted, all Scripture quotations are from the Holy Bible, New King James Version. Copyright © 2001 by Crossway Bibles, a division of Good News Publishers. Used by permission. Scripture quotations marked NASB are from the New American Standard Bible, copyright © 1960, 1962, 1963, 1968, 1971, 1972, 1973, 1975, 1977, 1995 by The Lockman Foundation. Used by permission. www.Lockman.org

Scripture quotations marked NIV are taken from the Holy Bible, New International Version®, NIV®. Copyright © 1973, 1978, 1984, 2011 by Biblica, Inc.® Used by permission of Zondervan. All rights reserved worldwide. www.zondervan.com. The "NIV" and "New International Version" are trademarks registered in the United States Patent and Trademark Office by Biblica, Inc.®

Copyright © 1982 by Thomas Nelson.
Used by permission.
All rights reserved.

Scripture quotations marked NLT are from the Holy Bible, New Living Translation, copyright © 1996, 2004, 2007. Used by permission of Tyndale House Publishers, Inc., Wheaton, IL 60189. All rights reserved.

Cover designed by: Marvin Eans, @marvineans.artanddesign

FOREWORD BY DANIEL KOLENDA

THE JOY OF PRAYER

MARK MOROZOV

CONTENTS

vi   Endorsements
ix   Foreword
xiii Acknowledgments

  1   Introduction
  4   Chapter 1: The Purpose, the Call
 20 Chapter 2: Remaining in Him
 34 Chapter 3: True Success
 46 Chapter 4: The Generals
 58 Chapter 5: Fasting and Praying
 70 Chapter 6: Three Types of Prayer
 92 Chapter 7: Call to Action
110 About the Author
111 Vision Statement
112 About the Ministry

THE JOY OF PRAYER ENDORSEMENTS

The Joy of Prayer is a transformative guide that reveals the profound ways in which prayer can bring true joy and fulfillment to our lives. With its insightful wisdom and practical strategies, this book unlocks the keys to success, helping readers discover the immense power of prayer in finding joy and achieving a meaningful Christian life.
—*Sid Roth, Sid Roth's It's Supernatural!*

Mark Morozov is an anointed messenger for this hour of history. The content of this book is birthed from the content and actual substance of his life. There is a language here that must provoke a lifestyle. There is an invitation in this book to be propelled into a deeper place of intimate fellowship with God, and by that, have your whole life and world transformed.
—*Michael Dow, Burning Ones Ministries, Habitation Church*

As clay to the seal receives its exact impression, so our hearts receive the joy of prayer through Mark's treatise.
—*Eric Gilmour, Sonship Intl*

Discover the transformative power of intimacy with God in this profound book. Through personal anecdotes and biblical teachings, Mark reminds us that true success doesn't always look like the way we define it. Love God, love your neighbor. The simplicity of this powerful book will cause you to re-evaluate everything. Prepare to be deeply moved and find the joy in prayer that will change your life forever.
—*Jeremy Johnson, Fearless LA Church*

Mark Morozov is a remarkable leader who is stewarding the call of God to his generation and ones to come!
–*Brian Barcelona, One Voice Student Missions, The Jesus Clubs, Gen-Z for Jesus*

As I read The Joy of Prayer, I felt a fresh desire stirring in my heart to find my mountain and be with Jesus. Mark is a pure voice who communicates the message of the Kingdom with such clarity. This generation lacks the spiritual depth that a life of prayer produces. As you read this book, the fire of First Love will burn in your heart—causing you to realign your priorities!
–*Matt Cruz, Matt Cruz Ministries*

The Joy of Prayer is a great book that will stir your prayer life and take it to the next level. Evangelist Mark Morozov shares truths from the Word of God and his personal experience that will increase your hunger for the Lord and take your prayer life to the next level as you read this book. I highly recommend it!
–*Chris Mikkelson, Chris Mikkelson Evangelistic Ministries*

I am stirred to pray! The Joy of Prayer will encourage you into an encounter with the Holy Spirit. The authentic truth that Mark conveys is essential for the church today. I can't wait for you to experience The Joy of Prayer.
—*Russ Benson, Christ for all Nations, Nations Church*

Through events in Mark's life, he has found the real treasure behind the door of the secret place. May we all be encouraged by his passion for prayer!
—*Weyman Dodson, Witness to the Nations*

The Joy of Prayer is an insightful, deep, and personal invitation to the place of communion with God. It stirs the heart and creates a hunger to walk closer with God. A truly inspirational book filled with truth.
—*David M. Remedios, Trinity Christian Center, Louisiana Outpouring*

Mark beautifully and ever so richly draws on scripture to enhance his Holy Spirit-inspired wisdom on the value, joy, and necessity of prayer. Intertwined with personal accounts, stories, and testimonies that undeniably stamp Mark and his ministry as authenticated by the Lord.
—*Scott McNamara, Jesus At The Door*

While turning the pages of Mark's book, The Joy of Prayer, you will find yourself being drawn into a greater dimension of revelation, discovering the possibilities, power, and potency of prayer. Every chapter will become a stepping stone for a deeper and stronger prayer life that will cause transformation to occur in you and through you!
—*Emanuel Rusu, Living Water Church*

The Joy of Prayer is the most transformational book for such a time as this. Through stories and practical insights, it will ignite a passion for prayer, leading you to discover the boundless joy in communion with God. It is a must-read book for every person who seeks to find true joy and meaning in life.
—*Vasiliy Yarosh, New Beginnings Church*

Someone once asked Evangelist John Wesley how he drew a crowd, and he reportedly said, "I set myself on fire, and people come and watch me burn." When I met Mark Morozov a few years ago, I was reminded of that quote. Mark is a man on fire, and you will feel the spiritual heat when you read his book, The Joy of Prayer. Mark understands that prayer flows out of a heart that is aflame with the Holy Spirit. Read this book and a spark will kindle an intense fire of intimacy and spiritual passion. Mark's message is contagious and I pray it will help ignite a revival.
—*Lee Grady, The Mordecai Project Ministry*

FOREWORD
By Daniel Kolenda

The time spent alongside the Master had left the disciples with an indelible impression of Jesus: He was a devoted prayer practitioner. Jesus often withdrew to quiet places where He could engage in uninterrupted communion with His Heavenly Father. While Jesus held great affection for His followers and undoubtedly felt the burden of ministry, His connection with His Father superseded all else in importance. The devotion to prayer embodied by Jesus was evident to His disciples. That's why, when the disciples approached Jesus with a request, they didn't ask, "Teach us to preach" or "Show us the way to cast out demons." Instead, their request was simple yet profound: "Lord, Teach us to pray."

This priority of Jesus' ministry has been the hallmark of extraordinary individuals throughout history—men and women of faith who unearthed the potent force of prevailing prayer. Charles Spurgeon said, "Prayer girds human weakness with divine strength, turns human folly into heavenly wisdom, and gives to troubled mortals the peace of God. We know not what prayer can do." John Wesley said, "God does nothing but in answer to prayer." The great pioneer missionary Adoniram Judson was known to withdraw from his friends and family seven times a day to pray alone. David Brainerd once wrote, "I love to be alone in my cottage where I can spend much time in prayer."

In this remarkable volume, "The Joy of Prayer," my dear friend Mark Morozov embarks on a journey into the heart of prayer. It's as if Mark, with an enthusiasm akin to a child discovering a treasure chest, invites us to step into the pages of his own life and encounter the transformative power of prayer.

FOREWORD

Mark's choice of this topic is no accident. In a world pulsating with confusing messages and priorities, he stands before us as a modern-day disciple, extending an invitation to join him, and the faithful through the ages, in exploring the path that Jesus Himself deemed paramount.

Starting with the heartbeat of our faith—the intimacy of our relationship with Christ—Mark unveils the truth that love births the most authentic and enduring endeavors. He beckons us into that hallowed sanctuary where the Father's heartbeat becomes our own guiding rhythm. Like a close friend leading us on an exhilarating journey, Mark reveals how prayer transforms us into willing co-travelers with God, following His lead, learning His desires, and discovering His will. Mark weaves in the stories of heroes of the faith, souls who blazed trails through time with their relentless pursuit of God's heart. We're reminded that we stand on the shoulders of giants, and prayer is the common thread that binds us to their legacy, inviting us to carry it forward into the realms of our own lives.

And what a life Mark has lived—a life scarred by loss, rejuvenated by redemption, and set ablaze by the fire of revival! As you journey through this book's pages, you'll understand that Mark isn't just an author; he's a living testament to the transformative power of prayer. His experiences, both triumphant and challenging, bear witness to a life that found its truest purpose and joy at the altar of God's presence.

So, dear reader, whether you're a seasoned prayer warrior or a seeker of spiritual truth, whether you've already tasted the sweetness of God's presence or are venturing into the secret place for the very first time, "The Joy of Prayer" invites you into a divine adventure, an exploration of the sacred union between the finite and the Infinite, the created and the Creator. So, embark on this journey with an open heart, a seeking spirit, and a readiness to discover the boundless joy that awaits you in the embrace of prayer.

Yours in the Gospel,

Daniel Kolenda
President and CEO of Christ for All Nations
Lead Pastor of Nations Church

ACKNOWLEDGMENTS

I would like to thank the people who have poured into my life and thus have influenced this book. I am eternally grateful for my family, friends, and the pastors who have molded my journey with God. You have helped me realize the magnitude of how important prayer is. Without your support, this book would not have been complete. Words cannot describe how much of an impact this has made, and this is just the beginning.

INTRODUCTION

Get ready to embark on the greatest journey of your life. Your destiny, purpose, and much more will be transformed by this subject. It truly changed my life, and it will do the same for you. There is joy in prayer, knowing your time is not wasted but invested—better than anything you can invest into on this earth. Many people don't realize the importance of this subject until the end of their lives. Many of the "greats" of our time only began digging the depths of what we are going to talk about later on in their journey. Let's not wait until it's too late.

As you read, do not feel the need to finish this book quickly. If the Holy Spirit pulls you away to close the pages and get alone with Him, please do so. This book is much more than the words that are written. The goal is for you to truly find the joy in prayer; to taste and see how good the Lord truly is. A life of prayer is not a chore—it is a delight. But no matter how many books you read, you will never truly understand this joy until you go into your secret place and get alone with God.

I will warn you now—everything will try to stop you from reading this book and receiving the full impartation that is available. Distractions will come and try to stop you from pausing and getting a glimpse of the beauty of Jesus. With just one glance, one touch from Him, your life will be changed forever. The enemy will try, but he will not prosper. I pray you will receive everything the Lord desires you to gain from these pages.

INTRODUCTION

I am praying for you to come out transformed, and that you will experience sudden visitations from the Holy Spirit. I promise you that by the end of this short book, you will notice shifts in your life. You will step into the new—Jesus makes all things new. There are divine moments with keys that help open the doors into deep intimacy with Jesus. I believe this book is full of those keys.

MARK MOROZOV

THE JOY OF PRAYER

ONE
THE PURPOSE, THE CALL

When I first started following Jesus, I tried really hard to find my purpose in life. I wanted to know what God had called me to do, where I was called to go, and what impact I was going to have on the world. Many people today are asking the same questions, but they are often confused about the answers. During this time when I was searching for my purpose and calling, I attended a conference where a very well-known evangelist was speaking.

During the conference, I approached him and asked him to pray for me. He asked, "What can I pray for?" I replied, "For me to find my purpose."

His answer wasn't what I was looking for, but it was what I needed to hear. The evangelist turned to me and said, "The will of the Father for you is to love the Father. It's to know the Father."

That moment marked my life forever. I was so busy looking for the purpose of God in my life when He was that purpose. I was busy looking for His hand and not His heart; therefore, I couldn't find His hand. But the moment I started looking for His heart, He trusted me with His hand. What do I mean by this? God's hand is His power, His strength, His activity in the world. I wanted to see His hand, that is, I wanted to be used by Him to win the lost, see signs and wonders, and "get the job done." But His heart is only found through intimacy.

FIRST LOVE

That's what it's all about: intimacy with Christ. You can save the whole world, but if you lose your soul, it's pointless. Our greatest purpose in life is to love Jesus. Sometimes we begin our journey with loving Jesus as the foundation only to leave that behind later on, as if it's a doorway to another purpose or just an entry point into our future. That is very dangerous. We should build our life on the foundation of Jesus and keep our relationship with Him the main thing. We must come to Him and seek Him for Him, not just so He will use us or help us accomplish some dream or vision we have received.

In the Book of Revelation, we read Jesus' messages to seven churches. One of these is the church in Ephesus. This church was "doing" a lot of work for God. Jesus tells them, "I know your works, your toil and your patient endurance...I know you are enduring patiently and bearing up for my name's sake, and you have not grown weary" (Rev. 2:2–3). They seemed to be fulfilling their calling, but there was one problem. Jesus then rebukes them by saying, "You have abandoned the love you had at first" (v. 4). They had lost sight of their greatest purpose and calling—to love Jesus. Don't let the work of the Lord distract you from the Lord of the work. When you seek Him, just come for Him. Seek the Father's heart. Cry out to know Him. Taste and see that He is good.

DON'T LET THE WORK OF THE LORD DISTRACT YOU FROM THE LORD OF THE WORK

In the natural, when you are hungry and eat, you become full. But it is the opposite with Jesus. If you are hungry for Him, when you seek and find Him you will become more hungry. When you are not hungry for Him, you should eat—only then will you become hungry again. When people ask me to pray for them to get a desire to seek God, I always ask, "When was the last time you prayed?" The answer is always, "Long ago." So eat His Word. Dig into the Scriptures. Get on your knees and open up your heart to the Lord like you would a friend, a parent, a mentor, or a spouse. The more you eat of His living bread, the hungrier you get for more bread. The more you drink of Him, the more thirsty you become.

> *But seek first the Kingdom of God and His righteousness,*
> *and all these things will be added to you.*
> *—Matthew 6:33*

When you seek the Lord first, everything else falls into place. The more I began to realize this in my own life, the more I fell in love with Him. The same can happen for you. The more you begin to realize this truth—that as you seek Him first He will provide all that you need—the more you will love Him. Many people do not seek God because they don't know what He is like. But when you start to discover Him more, you will find that you want more and more of Him. You will want to be with Him more because you have seen His goodness and all that He has for you as His son or daughter.

Billy Graham, perhaps the most famous evangelist of our time, was asked what he would do differently if he had to live his life over again. He responded, "I would study more. I would pray more, travel less, and take less speaking engagements. I took too many of them in too many places around the world... I'd spend more time in meditation and prayer and just telling the Lord how much I love Him and adore Him and [am] looking forward [to] the time we're going to spend together for eternity."[1] Even though he is now spending all of eternity with the Father, he still understood the importance of intimacy with God in this life.

Sadly, it's often at the end of someone's life that they realize the importance of fellowship with God and how much access they truly have to bring heaven on earth as they walk in the Spirit. When you are in an intimate relationship with the Father, seeing the things of heaven on earth is a reality. I don't want to be the person who lives for heaven but eventually realizes that he missed out on so much while living on this earth.

---

[1] Erin Roach, "Billy Graham, in TV Interview, Reflects: 'My Time Is Limited,'" Baptist Press, December 21, 2010, https://www.baptistpress.com/resource-library/news/billy-graham-in-tv-interview-reflects-my-time-is-limited/.

Take a moment to look at the apostles and the focus of their teaching toward the end of their lives. For many of them, their teaching in their later years was focused on their relationship with the Father. Paul said, "I count everything as loss because of the surpassing worth of knowing Christ Jesus my Lord" (Phil. 3:8).

Paul had all the ministry credentials and had seen many signs and wonders done through his hands, along with many people saved through his preaching. But Paul wanted one thing above all—to intimately know Jesus.

I also experienced something similar to this when I was close to death in a hospital in India. (See my first book, The Joy of Suffering, for the full story.) At that time, God told me He would heal me and that when I got home I was to seek His face. He did not tell me to go home and preach. I had one instruction: seek His face.

IT STARTS IN SECRET

If you seek God in secret, He will reward you in public. The reward God has for you in the public place is Him. He shows up. You begin to discern the voice of the Father above all other voices. There is no greater reward than this. This, in fact, is true joy. The power of God you want to see in your life or ministry needs to come from your secret place with Him. Everything you need to accomplish the purpose God has for you is accessed through a relationship with Jesus.

Everything you need to accomplish the purpose God has for you is accessed through a relationship with Jesus.

We can see this in the life of Moses, a man who had a great calling. Moses saw himself as incapable of being used by God because he had a stutter. But God essentially said to him, "Did I not create the mouth that you speak from?" (See Exodus 4:11.) If God had created his mouth, surely God could cause it to speak. Right? Moses asked God, "How will they know that You are with me?" God said, "What's in your hand?" Moses had a staff.

God told Moses to drop the staff, and it turned into a snake. Later on, God instructed Moses to perform this same miracle in front of Pharaoh. God didn't tell Moses to go and grab a slingshot and some rocks. This wasn't David meeting Goliath; it was Moses. God wanted a unique, personal relationship with Moses, so He used what Moses already had right in front of him. God will use what you already have, but He sometimes needs to reveal to you what it is that you have in your possession.

It is interesting that God did not initially show Moses the miracles in front of the people or in front of Pharaoh. It was first in the secret place where Moses was crying out to God that God showed him the miracle of the staff that he later used in front of the people. God took what Moses had experienced in private and rewarded him with the same manifestation in public.

Moses realized the importance of being with the Father. Everyone was afraid of going to the mountain to be with God, but Moses tasted and saw the goodness of God to the point that he said, "Unless Your presence goes with me, do not send me out of this place. What else will distinguish me from Your people?" (See Exodus 33:15–16.) Moses realized the importance of fellowship and the presence of the Father. It was that secret place that would change him and turn him into God's tool for His people. He experienced something in that place that was life—changing. Moses did not want to settle for what was normal, and he realized that having an experience with God was what would set him apart. You too can be set apart for the glory of God.

Everything I have experienced in my calling first began in the secret place. The Lord would show me the future when I was alone with Him. I saw things that were going to happen on the streets before they even happened. I would see myself traveling before I ever received an invitation or believed in myself to do what I do today. The same will happen for you. God will show you things to come from this moment forward.

HONDURAS TESTIMONY

I was asked to mentor a team that was traveling to Honduras for a mission trip. It was just a mentoring session to prepare the team before they went out to minister. I wasn't supposed to go with them, but as I met with the team, the Lord began to speak to my heart about going. Usually, the team would hold children's services at the schools in Honduras, but I knew there was more the Lord wanted me to do while I was over there. So I began to ask Him in a deeper way.

The Lord told me that I was to do a crusade there. I had attended several crusades before, but this would be the first one I would organize myself. I was very excited until I contacted a local organizer who had lived in Honduras for many years and shared the vision with him. He told me that what I was planning was impossible because of the rainy season, and that when they had tried to do events in the past, nobody showed up. I called some of the leaders of the missions groups from previous years and they told me the same thing—nobody showed up in the past, and it wouldn't work.

However, every time I went to the secret place, the Lord would assure me that this would work, even though everyone else said otherwise. He began to give me blueprints and strategies for what to do. One of the things He told me was to put posters everywhere a week before and promote the crusade on Facebook in a very specific way. He told me that people would pull off some of the flyers, but I should put them back up again three days before the crusade.

In the natural, it seemed like an impossible task. But we are called to live from the unseen realm. When we go into the secret place and spend time in prayer, we access this realm where we can receive heaven's strategies and plans. Without this reality, I would have never done what I did. So I decided to run with the vision God had given me.

I met with the pastors from several churches in Honduras to see whether they would help and partner with this vision. Together, we rented every chair we could find in the village where we were holding the crusade. To give you some perspective, the population of this village was around 100 people. But as instructed by the Lord, I decided to collect every chair in the city I could find—which ended up being over 500 chairs. I put them all out in faith because I knew the word that God had spoken to me in the secret place. I did everything exactly as He showed me. I silenced the outside voices and only took my commands from the secret place.

I had never done a crusade myself before, so I knew the Lord would have to take over. The crusade began at 6:00 p.m., but by then only three people had turned up. The organizer looked at me and said, "I told you." I looked at him and said, "No, they're coming—just watch."

At 6:15 p.m., several huge city buses started driving in. By 6:30, not only was every chair in the field filled but there were also many people out the back and outside of their houses standing all over the field. Many people parked their cars and motorcycles and stood watching and listening. Even the mayor of the city showed up. I later found out that she had been trying to stop the crusade from going ahead.

As I spoke, I talked about the healing power of God. The mayor came to the altar for prayer because she had cancer growing on her side. She started manifesting in front of all the people and was delivered. And the cancer on her side disappeared! She ended up testifying to all the people, and joy broke out in the crowd. Many people started running to the altar to get prayer and deliverance. It was the kind of service I had only ever read about in the Book of Acts. Many people were manifesting, getting delivered, and receiving healing.

When God tells you to do something, you do it with no questions asked.

But first, you have to access the unseen through a life of prayer so that God can speak to you. When God tells you to do something, you do it with no questions asked.

"While we do not look at the things which are seen, but at the things which are not seen. For the things which are seen are temporary, but the things which are not seen are eternal."
—2 Corinthians 4:18

Allow the reality of the unseen to become your reality today! The "seen" is temporary; one day it will all be gone. We will spend eternity in heaven or hell; therefore, the spiritual is more real and more important than the natural. The Father invites us to bring heaven on earth.

SMALL BEGINNINGS

I was once told a secret: "Do not despise small beginnings." It was from those small beginnings that I learned much of what I know today. If you cannot step out and tell one person about Jesus, how will you ever take radical steps for Him that result in thousands coming to know Him?

I didn't start out preaching at large events or crusades. I learned to step out in faith and flow in the gifts God had given me on the streets. Street evangelism is where I learned to be obedient to God's voice. But before street evangelism, it started in the secret place. It had to begin with the voice of God directing me to the people and places He had prepared for me. I have hundreds of testimonies of people who were saved because God was leading me every step of the way. It's not only for the streets.

I remember when I was selling cars, I promised God I would tell every person who came to look at the cars about Jesus. I sold over 85 percent of the cars to the first person who came to look at them. Many of us are afraid that if we give up control and let the Lord take over, we will not prosper, but I break that lie today in Jesus' name. You will prosper and succeed abundantly. Heaven's favor will be released as you release heaven's direction.

Obedience unlocks heaven on earth. How can you obey if you don't know the voice of the One whom you are obeying? It was in the secret place that I learned who God my Father is, and that my identity is in Christ and not in what I do. I paid attention to His voice in the secret place, and He rewarded me in public—the reward was His voice.

Find approval in God and no fear, rejection, doubt, or storm will stop or hinder you. Nothing will shake you because He will be your firm foundation. He will be the still, small voice that you follow. You will fall more in love with Him as you spend time with Him. It will not be a burden to serve Him, to find His call, or even to tell others about Him. You will not have to struggle to find your purpose. Whatever you do, you will do it for Him. It will all be from Him and through Him. Whether you are dealing with your business, career, ministry, family, church, or even ministering somewhere in the jungle, it will be a joy. There will be no striving because it will be God doing the work and not you.

God created us all, so only He can unlock each person so they may come to know Him. Learn to recognize His voice where it is quiet and He is the only One speaking. Let Him lead you with His still, small voice, and get ready for the greatest journey of your life.

I NEVER KNEW YOU

"Not everyone who says to Me, 'Lord, Lord,' shall enter the kingdom of heaven, but he who does the will of My Father in heaven. 22 Many will say to Me in that day, 'Lord, Lord, have we not prophesied in Your name, cast out demons in Your name, and done many wonders in Your name?' 23 And then I will declare to them, 'I never knew you; depart from Me, you who practice lawlessness!'"
—Matthew 7:21–23

This passage talks about the fact that many people will perform signs and wonders yet not go to heaven. Many people think that the will of the Father is to see signs, wonders, healings, and deliverance. These are an important part of our ministry—I would question those who do not have this fruit—but they are not the main thing.

Verse 21 says, "Not everyone who says to me, 'Lord, Lord,' shall enter the kingdom of heaven, but he who does the will of My Father in heaven". The next few verses tell us what the will of the Father is. We read, "Get away from Me; I never knew you, you who practice lawlessness." (See verse 23.) This verse states exactly what the will of the Father is for every follower: to know Jesus.

Our works becomes lawlessness when they are done without Jesus. Jesus says, "For without Me you can do nothing" (John 15:5). You can still do works on your own, but they will amount to nothing. It is possible for us to stand before Him and be told to get away because He never knew us. We might ask Him, "Didn't I prophesy in Your name?" but that won't be enough.

The problem is that many people today do works without God, causing more damage than good. This is why we see so much stress, pressure, anxiety, and so many fear-driven motives—and worst of all, jealousy, which only destroys people—in ministry, business, careers, and life in general. Many don't even realize they are bound by these things. This is not a competition; there are enough jobs for everyone. There are enough fish for everyone. Many souls need saving, so let's come together and see souls saved. Let's see growth in our finances, careers, and other areas of our lives. But these things are only done through union with Jesus. He knows how to advance you, and He wants to do it.

John G. Lake said, "The invitation is not 'Give Me thine head.' The invitation is, 'My son, give Me thine heart.' That is an affectionate relationship, a real love union in God. Think of the fineness of God's purpose. He expects that same marvelous spiritual union that is brought to pass between your soul and His own to be extended so that you embrace in that union every other soul around you."[2]

It's dangerous to go to church, attend services and revival meetings, and not have a personal relationship with Jesus. This is not just a warning for those who are seeing signs and wonders. Maybe today you are evangelizing and seeing fruit, but you haven't been with Him. My friend, that is lawlessness, and Jesus doesn't like it. It should never be about works; it should always be about Him. Works should flow out of your intimacy with Him.

---

[2] John G. Lake, "Christ Lives in Me—John G. Lake," Hope Faith Prayer, accessed March 28, 2023, https://www.hopefaithprayer.com/word-of-faith/christ-liveth-in-me-john-g-lake/.

This life of intimacy and obedience is available to everyone. Jesus desires to fill you and empower you with everything you need for this journey. As we end this chapter, I want to leave you with this powerful statement made by A.W. Tozer: "The great of the kingdom have been those who loved God more than others did."[3]

---

[3] A.W. Tozer, The Pursuit of God (Shippensburg, PA: Sea Harp Press, 2022), https://www.google.com/books/edition/The_Pursuit_of_God_Sea_Harp_Timeless_ser/peh8EAAAQBAJ?gbpv=1.

MARK MOROZOV

TWO
REMAINING IN HIM

*"As you therefore have received Christ Jesus
the Lord, so walk in Him."*
—*Colossians 2:6*

I want to talk a little bit about this verse from Colossians. But first let's rewind to the start to see what this book is all about. I love using my study Bible because it talks about the context of what was happening at the time when the Scriptures and letters were written. What was going on with the Colossians? My study Bible explains that it was the same thing that is happening in the body of Christ today: they were becoming distracted by many things. Many of the people from that body came from religious backgrounds. They began to mix things up and go back to their old, comfortable, religious ways. As they say, history repeats itself.

The church in Colossae was beginning to create its own theology rather than teach the true Gospel. Many were trying to pervert the Gospel. Since many of them had come from old religions, as they became distracted, the old wine was now coming back and mixing with the truth.

The enemy always wants us to pervert the Gospel, to remove its strength, because he knows there is power in the Gospel. He wants us to get caught up in our ideas, principles, and theologies, forgetting what the Word of God really says. He wants to place walls between us and the true purpose of God for our lives.

I pray that the Lord removes every wall that has slowed you down from pursuing Him. Paul's letter to the Colossians is a wake-up call for those Christians who have let their guard down and begun to compromise—a real slap in the face! He warns them, "Beware lest anyone cheat you through philosophy and empty deceit, according to the tradition of men, according to the basic principles of the world, and not according to Christ" (Col. 2:8).

Paul is essentially saying to them, "Listen, I want you to realize what's most important. You've lost the main thing. People are coming in and they're trying to teach you strange ideas, traditions." These teachers were trying to make the believers follow all kinds of rules and regulations, but Paul encouraged them to do one thing: walk in Christ. He was bringing them back to the most important thing. "As you therefore have received Christ Jesus the Lord, so walk in Him" (Col. 2:6). Therefore always means, "This is how you do it." Paul was saying, "Just as you have received Him, now walk in

Him." Jesus fulfilled the law and summed it up with one main first command: love God. If you love God, you will fulfill the rest of the commandments.

"For this reason we also, since the day we heard it, do not cease to pray for you, and to ask that you may be filled with the knowledge of His will in all wisdom and spiritual understanding; 10 that you may walk worthy of the Lord, fully pleasing Him, being fruitful in every good work and increasing in the knowledge of God; 11 strengthened with all might, according to His glorious power, for all patience and longsuffering with joy."
—*Colossians 1:9–11*

Paul says, "We've been praying for you, that you will be strengthened and refreshed so that you can continue to be pleasing in the Lord's sight." How? By remaining in Him.

"The mystery which has been hidden from ages and from generations, but now has been revealed to His saints. 27 To them God willed to make known what are the riches of the glory of this mystery among the Gentiles: which is Christ in you, the hope of glory."
—*Colossians 1:26–27*

Paul is saying there are some mysteries that are hidden for you to find in the Scriptures, in God, and with God. The mystery that was revealed to the Colossians was this: "Christ in you, the hope of glory" (v. 27). Let's keep diving into Colossians. "...in whom are hidden all the treasures of wisdom and knowledge."(Col. 2:3)

Do you know what wisdom is? I once asked the Lord, "What is wisdom? I want it." The Lord answered, "Walking in the Holy Spirit." He said, "I am wisdom. If you walk in Me, you will walk in wisdom." Wisdom is found only when we remain in Him.

"Beware lest anyone cheat you through philosophy and empty deceit, according to the tradition of men, according to the basic principles of the world, and not according to Christ."
—*Colossians 2:8*

There are many things in life that try to "cheat" you from abiding in Jesus. All hell will come against you to try and stop you from praying. Distractions will come your way. Your phone will start ringing, and your mind will wander. As Jesus calls you to go deeper with Him, you will have opportunities that may pull you away from Him. Your friends will invite you out to eat, but God will say, "No, I want you to go home." More business deals will come up, more ministry trips, new movies, social media, and many other things that can easily take you away from the Lord. How we respond in these situations will determine the depth of our relationship with Jesus.

Some of your friends might abandon you. But if your friends aren't praying, they aren't the people you need close to you. You can be around them to talk about Jesus, but I wouldn't keep them as your close friends because they're going to distract you from Him. You might lose some contracts. You might lose a relationship. Some ministry opportunities might disappear when you say yes to Jesus and no to earthly things. Trust me—those things are nothing compared to what you receive in Christ. The Lord will always reward you for what you have laid on the altar. The fire can only burn brighter when more logs are tossed into it.

The Lord will always reward you for what you have laid on the altar. The fire can only burn brighter when more logs are tossed into it.

In the Old Covenant, only certain people from a certain tribe were able to be priests and enter into the holy of holies, which is the presence of God. The priest would enter the Tabernacle and go through different cleansing rituals before he could enter the holy of holies. If he was in sin when he entered, he would fall down and die. The priest would have a rope tied around his leg and a little bell attached to him so that if he fell and died, the people would hear the ringing of the bell and pull the priest out using the rope.

But everything changed when Jesus paid the price for us on the cross, shedding His blood and dying the death you and I should have died. We know John 3:16 "For God so loved the world that He gave His only begotten Son, that whoever believes in Him should not perish but have everlasting life." Because of Jesus' sacrifice for us on the cross, now we all have access to the holy of holies. It's not just the priest, not just a spiritual leader, but everybody who can now enter and fellowship with God.

We don't have to sacrifice any kind of blood because Jesus' blood has been poured over everything. Now we are always able to enter into the presence of God.

Paul is taking the Colossians back to this: "Just as you have received Him, walk in Him." (See Colossians 2:6.) Let's have a look at how other translations present this verse:

NIV: "Continue to live your lives in him."
NLT: "Continue to follow him."

Remain connected to God. Remain plugged into Him. Follow Him just as you did before. Stay with Him.

You can read half the Bible and still be addicted to pornography, video games, gossip, pride, control, or manipulation. But I'm going to tell you how to get free: Don't come to God to be free. Come to Him for Him. When you come to Jesus and you show up and begin to pray and seek Him, all the other gods in your life must crumble—but not because you destroyed them, because you can't. The Father knew that. That's why He sent Jesus. But when you abide in Him, all those high things come down.

If you're addicted to anything, if you have some kind of jealousy or envy toward somebody, if you struggle with gossip, or if you're just not hungry for Jesus, come to Him. I said it earlier, but it's worth saying again: In the natural, if you eat, you are no longer hungry. But in the spiritual, when you eat, you become more hungry. Some of you lack hunger because you have not been eating spiritual food.

Just show up. Start with five minutes a day. Then you can slowly increase your time. Don't stay the same; grow in your relationship with God. You are always either moving forward or going backward. There's no "taking a season off" or taking a vacation from Jesus. If you stop your pursuit, you will find yourself drifting. We need God, which is why Paul tells us to "walk in Him." That's what will hold, protect, and propel you into everything Jesus has for you.

Don't stay the same; grow in your relationship with God. You are always either moving forward or going backward.

A good majority of today's problems are the result of people not abiding. Many of us have given our lives to Jesus, but we've stopped pursuing Him. We have not continued the Christian life. Perhaps we have become so comfortable in our salvation that we feel like we don't need to seek Him anymore. But the true fruit of our salvation is remaining in Him.

HE WHO HAS THE SON

I once heard a story about an old, wealthy man. This man had many possessions. He liked collectibles, particularly from shipwrecks. He liked to collect things like paintings, golden cups, and old chariots worth millions of dollars.

When this man died, all his possessions were taken to be auctioned off. Everybody in the town, then in the city, and then in the world began to find out about this man and the items being sold. Many museums had been trying to get a hold of these items, but they were now being auctioned off to all kinds of people from different countries.

Everybody was excited to bid at the auction. The first item that was up for sale was a painting. It wasn't a famous painting but one of the deceased man's son that he painted himself. The man loved his son, and when the young boy died, he painted a picture of him to remember him by. Nobody was interested in this painting; they were all after the golden cup, or the painting of Mona Lisa, or another item from a shipwreck.

When a little old man in the back put down the first bid for the painting, everyone laughed at him for bidding on such an insignificant item. The painting was sold to the man in the back for only $10. Straight away, however, the auctioneer announced that the auction was over. Everyone was confused, as they still had their eyes on many of the other items. The auctioneer then explained that according to the will of the man who had died, whoever bought the painting of his son would get everything else as well. The old man in the back had just won the biggest lottery of his life, and he hadn't even come for all the other things. He had come for the one painting.

He who has the Son has everything. If you leave with anything after reading this book, may you leave with your eyes on Jesus. Some of us are running after other things. We're trying to run after the golden cup or some other treasure. Some of us are chasing open doors, the next relationship, the next business deal, or whatever the latest trend is. But in doing so, we are forsaking Him. This is what makes Christianity different from every other religion: Jesus wants you to know Him intimately. Knowing that is true joy. Knowing Him is true joy.

> **If you leave with anything after reading this book, may you leave with your eyes on Jesus.**

Sometimes we think that being born again is it—after that, we're done. But no, it goes much further. When we surrender our lives, we say, "Yes, Jesus. It's no longer I who live." We're put in a grave. We're dead now. It is Christ who lives in us. But then we have to walk in Him.

You see, the difference between religion and relationship is this: Religion says, "I'm going to do everything I can to try to earn what I can from God." Sometimes this looks like trying to read the Word every single morning just to check it off your list. But a true relationship says to Jesus, "I'm here for You." Pursue Jesus to love Him, not because you have to in a religious way. True love for Him will bring you back. If there is no love, ask Him to help you.

Jesus understood we couldn't do it on our own—that's why He came. He died so that we could find true life in Him through the Holy Spirit. Stop trying to live this life on your own. Surrender. Let go and give Jesus control. Allow Him to be the Lord of your life, ministry, career, family, business, relationships, church, and your prayer life.

Some of you don't have an appetite anymore because you've stopped eating. You've stopped digging into the Scriptures; you've stopped reading; you've stopped studying—you've stopped looking for Him. You might think that you've done enough by memorizing John 3:16, but every time you read it, a new layer gets peeled back. Every time you read the Word, a spiritual sifting is going on within you. There's a cutting away. God is doing something every time.

You might not feel it; you might not know it. You might know every word of the Bible. But I'm telling you, keep reading. Even when you do know a Scripture verse, keep reading it because something is happening in the background that you don't know about.

Some of you have been praying, "God, I want the anointing. I want the fire. When I speak, I want You to show up." When I come into a worship setting and I don't feel the tangible presence of God, I know that the worship leaders haven't been praying. When I come into a service and I don't feel the tangible presence of God as the preacher is ministering, I know he or she has not been with Jesus.

Prayer unlocks heaven on earth. When you seek God in secret, He will reward you in public. And the reward He gives is Himself: His glory, His voice, His fire. You do not need to be jealous of the fire on someone else—you can access it for yourself. The Holy Spirit fell on each of the disciples at Pentecost, and He wants to fall on you. There is a unique blessing and calling for your life. Don't live with jealousy toward others, but seek to be the best person you can be: you, in Him.

PRESSING FORWARD

Jesus is calling us to connect to the Vine. This is not a once-in-a-lifetime event. It's not saying, "Yes, Jesus, I'll follow You," and then going home and that's it. It's a daily pursuit after Him. It's daily saying, "Yes, I do." And as we say yes to Him, we say no to our flesh. We die to our selfish desires.

Some of you started praying, but you stopped because you didn't want to die to yourself. Why do I say that? Because when we show up to pray, God often starts showing us what is really in our hearts. He might ask you to pray more or to wash your wife's dishes occasionally. He might say, "I want you to forgive this person," or, "You're gossiping. I want you to stop gossiping." And so you leave the secret place after five minutes because you feel uncomfortable due to the conviction of the Holy Spirit as you prayed. Your flesh doesn't like it, so it pulls you away from the secret place. (Please read that again in case you missed it.) But when you choose to remain with Jesus, you start getting His characteristics: love, joy, peace, and so much more.

We stop remaining in Jesus when we stop walking with Him. Walking requires us to move forward. The life we are called to live is not a passive one where we say yes to Jesus and then stop. You have to keep moving forward, seeking Him with all your heart.

When you're wearing the armor of God, it covers your front. You have the sword of the Spirit, the breastplate of righteousness, the shield of faith, the belt of truth, and the shoes of the Gospel. (See Ephesians 6:10–18.) Your whole front is covered, but your back isn't. So in our Christian walk, we're called to pioneer forward—to keep on praying, keep pursuing the Lord. Even when it's hard, when we're tired and busy, we push forward to seek Him so we can know Him deeper.

What if you don't have the desire to pray? Where do you start? How do you get the hunger back if it's no longer there? The answer is simple: just show up. Give God one minute if that's all you've got and tell Him exactly what you are feeling: "Lord, I'm not hungry for You. I was when I first met You, but my love for You isn't there anymore." Then the next day, show up for two minutes. The day after, show up for three minutes, then four, five, ten, thirty minutes. You will notice that a year has gone by and you're now spending an hour with Him—and you'll be hungry for more!

Let's not leave God in a church building. Let's not leave Him in a closet. Let's not leave Him in some upstairs prayer room. Let's remain in Him. The disciples were around Jesus every day. They saw Him pray, yet they turned to Him and said, "Teach us to pray." They saw something different in Jesus. They saw that Jesus only did what the Father told Him to do. Jesus remained in His Father.

Let's not leave God in a church building. Let's not leave Him in a closet. Let's not leave Him in some upstairs prayer room. Let's remain in Him.

If something is slowing you down—social media, video games, or other activities—lay it down. I've spent periods of time off social media, not because I have an issue with it, but because I just want more of God.

Maybe you can't get rid of greed relating to your finances. Maybe you can't get rid of gluttony—you just love food. Come to God quickly. Seek Him. Cry out to Him. Tell Him honestly how you are doing. Don't hold anything back.

Ask Him, "God, what is it that is holding me from You? What is it that You want me to lay down tonight so I can remain in You, so I can go deeper with You?" Maybe He has something new for you. Seeking God is like peeling back an onion—every season, He peels back a new layer and reveals more of His heart to you.

My life was completely changed when I learned to abide in

the Lord. I had plans; I had everything laid out, what I thought I was going to do. But you know what? I didn't know what God was calling me to do until I started to abide in Him. My true life started when I began to pray. I started to seek Him. I sometimes pulled my car over to simply thank the Lord. I started to worship Him, and as I did, He began to reveal to me my identity and show me my purpose. I began to live. I absolutely love life now, and I wouldn't want to do anything else other than walk in Him. And He wants to do the same for you.

MARK MOROZOV

THREE
TRUE SUCCESS

What is true success? Many of us imagine having a successful business or ministry, and we pray that God will give us success in these areas. But true success is not in the numbers, or the profit, or the size of your career, business, family, or your ministry. Remember what the man of God told me: "The will of God for you is to love God."

Loving God is success. When I realized this, I stopped looking for what I could do for God and began to look for Him. If you want to be great in this life, find out what Jesus thinks is the greatest. He created you as beautiful, talented, and gifted for a very specific reason and calling. Wouldn't you want Him to reveal all that He has created you for? He desires this more than you know.

THE GREATEST COMMANDMENT

> *"And behold, a lawyer stood up to put him to the test, saying, 'Teacher, what shall I do to inherit eternal life?' 26 He said to him, 'What is written in the Law? How do you read it?' 27 And he answered, 'You shall love the Lord your God with all your heart and with all your soul and with all your strength and with all your mind, and your neighbor as yourself.' 28 And he said to him, 'You have answered correctly; do this, and you will live.'"*
> —Luke 10:25–28

In this story from Luke 10, a lawyer approached Jesus with a question: "What must I do to inherit eternal life?" Jesus didn't answer him directly, but replied with a question: "What is written in the Law?" The lawyer answered, "To love the Lord your God with all your heart and with all your soul and with all your strength and with all your mind, and your neighbor as yourself." This lawyer was correct, so Jesus told him to follow this command.

There are two laws here:
1. Love the Lord your God.
2. Love your neighbor.

If you follow these two laws, you fulfill the rest of the Law. If you love God and your neighbor, you will not want to commit adultery, steal, murder, or covet.

The number one law is to love the Lord—not only to love Him, but to love Him with all of your heart, mind, soul, and strength. This is completely falling in love with Jesus, surrendering all of ourselves to Him. When we do this, Christ is formed in us.

We will never succeed by trying hard to do all the right things. It's only by the grace of God and through the power of the Holy Spirit we can fulfill our calling. Mankind has always tried to follow the law in its own strength but has always failed. But now, because we have Christ in us, we don't have to rely on ourselves.

The Holy Spirit helps us to love God with all of our hearts. If you focus on doing everything perfectly, and checking all the boxes, you will find yourself constantly struggling. But if you truly love Jesus with all your heart, mind, soul, and strength, you will want to do the things He says. You will want to pray, fast, and seek Him with all your heart. There is nothing greater than truly loving Jesus. As you do this, you will not be able to hold Him in—He will overflow to others around you. You will find yourself talking about the One you are truly in love with. Your whole life will be centered around this One.

If you want to love Jesus more, spend more time in His presence. Be filled daily with the Holy Spirit. Galatians 5:16 says, "But I say, walk by the Spirit, and you will not gratify the desires of the flesh." It's the Spirit that will enable you to say no to the world and the flesh. But if you are not filled daily with the Holy Spirit, you may be like the people Paul described to Timothy, "having the appearance of godliness, but denying its power" (2 Tim. 3:5). There's nothing scarier than assuming you are walking rightly with God when you are actually missing Him and the power of the Holy Spirit He has to offer you. So many believers will get to heaven and realize they missed out on so much that was available while they were on Earth.

This power is found in God's presence. If you have chaos in your job, you will find victory in His presence. If you have depression in your home, you will find joy in His presence. But instead, we fill our time with other things: watching TV, playing video games, chasing success and material things, relationships, and more. These things can be distractions from the pain and lack that we feel in our hearts. They are not necessarily bad until they begin to hold a higher place in our lives than Christ Himself.

If you have lost that fellowship with Jesus today, go back to what's most important—your love for Him. In Revelation, Jesus called the church in Ephesus to return to the love that they once had (Rev. 2:4). If you have lost your first love for Him, now is the best time to return. I believe this powerful A.W. Tozer quote will bless you: "The instant cure of most of our religious ills would be to enter His presence."[4]

Begin to love Him for Him, and you will watch God come and move powerfully through your life. I have seen so many believers get caught up in the busyness of life and lose their love for God Himself. They still do many things for His name's sake, but not with Him. He wants a union with you. He wants intimacy. Even more than just wanting it, the Spirit inside you is crying out, "Abba, Father." He is wisdom. Jesus is true success.

The first and greatest commandment is to love God, but Jesus adds a second law—love your neighbor. There is a reason why these two commands appear together. If you truly love the Lord your God, you're going to love your neighbor. Loving your neighbor is a test to show if you truly love God and are walking in the Holy Spirit. If you

---

[4] A.W. Tozer, "A.W. Tozer Quotes," Quotefancy.com, accessed March 28, 2023, https://quotefancy.com/a-w-tozer-quotes.

can't love your neighbor whom you do see, how can you love God whom you do not see? John said this in his first letter:

> *"If anyone says, 'I love God,' and hates his brother, he is a liar; for he who does not love his brother whom he has seen cannot love God whom he has not seen. 21And this commandment we have from him: whoever loves God must also love his brother."*
> *—1 John 4:20–21*

If you truly love the Lord your God, you're going to love your neighbor.

THE GOOD SAMARITAN

In his conversation with the lawyer, Jesus goes on to tell a story that many of you will be very familiar with—the story of the Good Samaritan.

> *"A man was going down from Jerusalem to Jericho, when he was attacked by robbers. They stripped him of his clothes, beat him and went away, leaving him half dead."*
> *—Luke 10:30, NIV*

This story takes place on a busy road from Jerusalem to Jericho. What happened to the man in this story was probably not uncommon. People would get beaten up by robbers often, and the priests and Levites who regularly walked by would do nothing. Nobody else was doing anything about the situation, so these religious leaders decided not to do anything either. The Bible says they both "passed by on the other side" (v. 31, NIV). These leaders were not considering God's purposes for them; they were simply going along with what was "common" at the time. And in doing so, they were setting a bad example for the people who looked up to them. How many things do we do today because they are the "common" thing? Do we make excuses because "everybody does that"? I pray that the Holy Spirit would highlight those things to you as you read this book.

> *"But a Samaritan, as he traveled, came where the man was; and when he saw him, he took pity on him. 34 He went to him and bandaged his wounds, pouring on oil and wine. Then he put the man on his own donkey, brought him to an inn and took care of him."*
> *—Luke 10:33–34, NIV*

There's something in this story that is embarrassing: it wasn't the priest or the Levite—the religious people—who stopped and helped the man in need. It was the Samaritan man who helped this Jewish man. Samaritans and Jews were in conflict with each other at the time.

Sometimes it seems like the world knows how to show more love than the average believer. No wonder so many people want nothing to do with the body of Christ. But not your generation—this generation the Lord is raising up is different.

At the end of this story, Jesus tells the lawyer to "go and do likewise" (Luke 10:37). The lawyer knew the Law—he knew what he had to do—but he was not doing it. We know that we need to love God. We know we need to love our neighbor. But the question is, what do we do about it? Do we forgive those who wrong us? Are we helping those in need? Are we like the priest or like the Samaritan? Do we just know the Word of God, or do we put it into practice? May we not just be hearers of the Word, but doers. May we set others above ourselves and not be those who are "lovers of self" (2 Tim. 3:2).

LOVE AND UNITY

When we truly love God first, it will be His love that fills us and His love that we have toward our neighbor. We need this love in the body of Christ now more than ever. The enemy knows the strength of our unity, and he seeks to destroy it. I believe that true unity will release the end-time revival that is coming.

True unity will release the end-time revival that is coming. There's a reason Jesus split the fivefold ministry into five parts. To manifest His fullness we must be able to put aside our differences and work together, complementing each other's strengths, not destroying each other because of our weaknesses. We would have major problems if we were all created the same. So if each of us will spend time in God's presence and learn to love Him for Him, we will see so much more love for one another in the body of Christ and our communities.

Genesis 11 tells a story about the people of the earth coming together to try and build a tower to heaven. The Bible says the Lord saw that they were "one people" and that "nothing that they propose to do will now be impossible for them" (Gen. 11:6). God came down and mixed up their languages so they were not in one accord because their purpose wasn't in line with His plan for the world.

Do you realize how much we can achieve as the church if we come together instead of holding on to offense and destroying one another? There's strength in the unity of the body of Christ. Why does the devil often attack our families? Why does he try to cause division among the churches and denominations? It's because he knows that when we come together, there's no stopping what God can do.

When we come together, there's no stopping what God can do. There are many examples throughout Scripture of the power and necessity of unity in the kingdom of God.

Ecclesiastes 4:12 says, "And though a man might prevail against one who is alone, two will withstand him—a threefold cord is not quickly broken." God is calling us to come together in love for one another. And as we do, the world will come into our churches and recognize the love of God among us. The Word of God says, "By this all people will know that you are my disciples, if you have love for one another" (John 13:35). People will come and they will want to stay when they see this unity.

Early in His ministry, Jesus cast demons out of many people, and the Pharisees were not happy. They accused Jesus of being "possessed by Beelzebul" and casting out demons "by the prince of demons" (Mark 3:22). Jesus replied, saying, "How can Satan cast out Satan? If a kingdom is divided against itself, that kingdom cannot stand. And if a house is divided against itself, that house will not be able to stand" (vv. 23–25).

The enemy knows this reality, that when he can turn people against each other and get them fighting for position, getting jealous, making false accusations, and taking offense, they can't walk in everything God has called them to.

Matthew 5:23–24 says, "So if you are offering your gift at the altar and there remember that your brother has something against you, leave your gift there before the altar and go. First, be reconciled to your brother, and then come and offer your gift." Power is released when we forgive each other and join in unity.

In the Book of Acts, the believers were waiting for the Holy Spirit "with one accord" (Acts 1:14). He came when they were in unity with one another. May we put away selfish desires and walk in wholeness with one another. Together we will see revival in our generation. There will be one main goal that will bring the body together, and that is Jesus. When He is the center once again, He will bring all men to Himself.

DEATH TO SELF

The only way we can truly come together in unity and love for one another is to die to ourselves. Our walk with God is not just a confession; it's a daily walk of death to self. Jesus said, "If anyone would come after me, let him deny himself and take up his cross daily and follow me" (Luke 9:23). This is the only way for us to be separate from this world. But if we hold on to our selfish desires, building our empires and drawing attention to ourselves, we will only cause division in the body of Christ, which will lead to a powerless church.

When we confessed Jesus as our Lord, we were baptized into His death. Our old selves passed away, and all things were made new. But we have to walk in daily denial of self, coming into the light and seeing Him face to face. Again, the answers are found when you embrace the true joy of prayer. It's when you come into the light of His presence that you die. Your desires die. Your sin dies. Your old nature dies. In His presence, God reveals to you hidden sins that are hindering you from living as you should. As you confess these sins, die to yourself, and get filled with His life, you become more and more like Him.

This is the glorious life that Jesus offers us. A life where we are dead to ourselves and alive to Christ, so that we can become living bread to a dying world. So fix your eyes on the author and perfecter of our faith (Heb. 12:2, NASB) and let Him transform you in His presence as you seek His face.

A SUCCESSFUL LIFE

Jesus gives us these two commands—love God and love your neighbor. This is what it looks like to be successful in the Christian life. At the end of the story, Jesus says to the lawyer, "Go and do likewise." Don't waste time on this. Don't just know the Word. Jesus told this story to encourage us to go and live by the Word, putting it into practice. Make a decision to start today. Make the choice that loving God will be your highest purpose in life, and watch as the power of God begins to manifest in your life like never before.

You will not have to struggle to love your enemy; it will be natural. It will be the Father in you, loving them. The power of God inside you will fill your life so that you can forgive those who persecute you for Jesus' sake. It will fill you to love those who irritate you at work or to love those who might be a little weirder than you.

My religious sensor goes off when I am spending time with the Lord but not loving my neighbor. At these times, I realize that my prayer time is religious, repetitive, and not relational. If you are truly in relationship with Jesus, you will love your neighbor.

Check where your walk with Jesus is today. Are there people you cannot talk to? Do you have family members you ignore? Are there church leaders you have rejected because of mistakes they have made? Get alone with Jesus today and let Him take these burdens from you. Let the power of God consume you so that you live out the reality of what you believe.

> ***Let the power of God consume you so that you live out the reality of what you believe.***

In the Luke 10 story we read, the priest and the Levite knew that it was right to help the man in need but did nothing. It was the Samaritan who helped the Jew who had been robbed and beaten. So many people know the Word and can quote Scripture passages but do not have the power to live it out. Jesus wants to give us the power of the Holy Spirit so that we can live out what we know. That's the difference between the law and the Spirit.

May you see by the Spirit as you read these pages. May He reveal to you where you truly stand so that you can ask for forgiveness where it is needed. Then take action. Meet with people and restore relationships.

Do what you can to make peace with people. Don't just stay where you are. This could be the very thing that has hindered your relationship with the Lord. Don't get stuck in the wilderness, but advance with the Lord. Pass your test. Let those walls come down.

MARK MOROZOV

FOUR
THE GENERALS

There are many men and women whose prayer lives are an example for us to follow. Several books have been written about these men and women of God. But of course, we should start this chapter out with the greatest General that ever lived and walked this earth—Jesus Himself. Even Jesus, fully God and fully man, needed to have a prayer life. We read that many times He would disappear from His disciples to go and seek the Father on a mountain or in some secret place. Jesus didn't only talk about prayer—He lived it. If Jesus needed to pray, how much more do we need to?

Jesus' prayer life was so significant that the disciples who walked with Him and saw all of His miracles and His ministry wanted one thing more than any other: to learn His life of prayer. They asked Him, "Lord, teach us to pray" (Luke 11:1).

The disciples prayed, but they didn't see the success Jesus had. They saw that there was something different about the way Jesus prayed. What was that difference? Jesus actually fellowshipped with the Father. He didn't just pray a prayer as some religious routine or repetitive religious words. Jesus spoke with the Father as if the Father was right in front of Him.

We need to look to Jesus to really know what it looks like to have a prayer life—what it looks like to have real fellowship with the Father. Jesus said these words: "Truly, truly, I say to you, the Son can do nothing of his own accord, but only what he sees the Father doing. For whatever the Father does, that the Son does likewise" (John 5:19). He had the success, the breakthrough, and the answers only because He did what the Father told Him to do.

Jesus was totally in sync with the Father. That's what Jesus came for. He didn't give His life only so that our sins could be forgiven. It wasn't just so His Spirit could enter us and we could walk in the authority that He freely gives to us. It was to give us access to the Father while we are here on this earth so we can experience the kingdom of God, as the Bible says, "on earth as it is in heaven" (Matt. 6:10). The way that we access heaven is through Jesus.

This was God's original design for mankind. The Bible talks about how in the beginning, Adam and Eve walked and talked with God. They had an intimate relationship with God. But after they disobeyed God, and ate from the tree of the knowledge of good and evil, sin entered mankind.

The flesh is now a sinful flesh, and the sinful flesh distances us from fellowship with God. In the Old Testament, you see man trying to restore that fellowship with the Father over and over again, but they kept falling short; they kept messing up. So God had a plan of redemption: He sent Jesus down to earth. Jesus came and gave His life for us on the cross so that we could be restored to what we had in the Garden of Eden, restored to that fellowship with God.

Now we have access to the Father through Jesus. We have died with Him. It's no longer us who live, but Christ who lives in us—the hope of glory. As we die with Him, our new man will resurrect with Him as well. We will walk with Him on this earth, and accomplish His purposes, and His destiny in and through our lives. This can only be done when we are fully in sync with the Spirit of God, just as Jesus was when He walked this earth. There were places where Jesus went and had great success, where miracles, signs, and wonders followed Him, only because the Father had led Him there.

The Father wants to lead you in that same way today. He wants to use you to do the miraculous. This can only be done through an intimate relationship with Him. The Bible tells us to seek the Father in secret and He will reward us in public (Matt. 6:6–7).

When you've sought the Father in the secret place, where nobody sees, where it's just you and Him, the doors closed, you lean in and hear the voice of the Shepherd calling. As you spend more time with Him, you understand more of who He is. You begin to understand His heart. You learn to understand and discern His voice—His still, small voice. Then, when you're in public amongst the noise, chaos, and confusion, you are still able to hear Him because you have learned His voice in secret.

This is just like a couple who has spent so much time together that all they need to do is smile to communicate with each other. They can laugh without saying anything. And each of them knows what the other is thinking because they've spent time with each other. The same is true with Jesus. As you spend more time with Him, you will begin to know His heart in public. It was never just about praying a simple prayer of confessing your sins and asking Jesus to come into your heart. It was always about walking with the Father daily.

I think our body of Christ today has watered down this truth, and so we have a powerless Christianity. We have so many men who know of God, but do not walk with God. We have powerless motivational preachers holding fruitless services—this has become normal. If most of these preachers really walked with God, their lives would reveal the fact that they have been with Jesus.

We see this in the lives of the disciples. When they spent time with Jesus, they went out and preached with boldness, and people saw the difference in their lives. Even though they were uneducated men, because of their boldness, the people knew that they had been with Jesus. It was the fruit of intimacy with Jesus that was seen in public.

The enemy does not want you to seek the Father. The enemy wants to cause you to be busy and distracted with other things so that you miss Jesus in the room. But if you will turn aside, get alone like Jesus did, and seek your Father, you will begin to see the fruitfulness that Jesus saw in His life and ministry.

BILLY GRAHAM

Billy Graham was a general who left a huge impact on the world, like many others who gave their lives away to follow the call of Jesus. I have already mentioned him in this book, but it's worth remembering the answer he gave when asked if there was anything he would do differently if he had the chance: "I would study more. I would pray more, travel less, take less speaking engagements…I'd spend more time in meditation and prayer and just telling the Lord how much I love Him and adore Him and [am] looking forward [to] the time we're going to spend together for eternity."[5]

Even though Billy Graham is going to spend eternity in heaven with the Father, he realized the value of having a relationship with the Father while still on this earth. So many people only realize this at the very end of their lives. Why not take hold of this now? Don't wait until your life is nearly over.

CHARLES FINNEY

The next person I want to talk about is Charles Finney. Finney was a revivalist who was used by God during the Second Great Awakening in America. When he started holding revival meetings in Rochester, New York, which was a small city at the time, not many people knew about him.

What many people don't know is that before Finney ever showed up, a man named Daniel Nash would come to the grounds and begin praying and interceding for a move of God. This man, known to many as Father Nash, dedicated his life to the ministry of Charles Finney. Father Nash would arrive two or three weeks before a revival meeting and begin to pray. When he felt in his spirit that the time was right, he would reach out to Finney and tell him the grounds were ready to hold the meetings.

---

[5] Roach, "Billy Graham, in TV Interview, Reflects: 'My Time Is Limited.'"

When Charles Finney arrived in Rochester, New York, there was a tangible presence of God over that area. Young kids began to weep and cry in their schools for seemingly no reason, only because they began to feel the conviction of their sin. Their teachers didn't know what to do, and they had to call Charles Finney in because they needed help. He would preach the Gospel, and these young kids would give their lives to Jesus.

There was such an outpouring of the Holy Spirit during this time, and the tangible presence of God was felt all over. Several businesses closed down. Bars and strip clubs closed down. Many people moved to Rochester, and the city's population multiplied by about three. Signs and wonders were taking place, and the news was spreading everywhere by word of mouth. There was such conviction in the area that people were not committing crimes anymore. Police officers had nothing to do. No one was robbing, stealing, or killing. Talk about the church being the light driving out darkness!

Charles Finney's ministry was held together by this intercessor who was standing in the gap for him—Father Nash. When Father Nash passed away, it wasn't long before Charles Finney's ministry closed, where he then became a local pastor. His itinerant ministry stopped because it had been held together in the spirit by this powerful intercessor.

That's the power of prayer and intercession. The Bible says that we're in a fight. It's not against flesh and blood but against spiritual principalities (Eph. 6:12). There is a fight in the spirit over America. There's a fight in the spirit over this territory. We need people to rise up and hear what heaven is saying and do what heaven is doing, on earth.

If many of us began to truly rise up and pray, how many more Charles Finneys would we have today? Will you be the next Father Nash or Charles Finney of your generation?

GEORGE MÜLLER

George Müller was a Christian evangelist and the director of the Ashley Down Orphanage in Bristol, England, as well as one of the founders of the Plymouth Brethren movement. Müller was a mighty man of God who was led by prayer. He was a man who stood in the gap. He started a huge orphanage with thousands of young kids that were saved from the streets, whom he helped get on their feet. He was a man who prayed for everything. He would pray for the orphans, the food, and every provision that he needed to continue to keep the orphanage afloat.

Müller never asked anyone for money—he just prayed and trusted God to provide for everything. There was a time when the orphanage had no money and Müller prayed for God to bring food so he could feed the orphans. After he prayed, he heard a knock on the front door. When he opened the door, there was nobody there, but there were several bags of groceries full of food—just enough to feed him and the orphans.[6]

This was the way Müller lived. He famously said, "Faith does not operate in the realm of the possible. There is no glory for God in that which is humanly possible. Faith begins where man's power ends."[7] Many of us would never take the steps of faith that Müller

---

[6] "George Müller: Trusting God for Daily Bread," Harvest Ministries, accessed March 28, 2023, https://harvestministry.org/muller.

[7] George Müller, "George Müller Quotes," Quotefancy.com, accessed March 28, 2023, https://quotefancy.com/quote/1337131/George-M-ller-Faith-does-not-operate-in-the-realm-of-the-possible-There-is-no-glory-for.

did. He saw God provide everything from clothes for the kids to the houses and the buildings they lived in.

The Bible tells us that if we ask for anything that is according to God's will, it will be done for us. Yes, I believe there are times when God will call you to humble yourself, go low, and ask people for help. Müller's first response was always to run straight to God. He believed that all you have to do is ask God, and God will provide everything. He had a miraculous gift of faith.

THE NAZIRITES

> *"And the LORD spoke to Moses, saying, 2 'Speak to the people of Israel and say to them, When either a man or a woman makes a special vow, the vow of a Nazirite, to separate himself to the LORD, 3 he shall separate himself from wine and strong drink. He shall drink no vinegar made from wine or strong drink and shall not drink any juice of grapes or eat grapes, fresh or dried. 4 All the days of his separation he shall eat nothing that is produced by the grapevine, not even the seeds or the skins.'"*
> —Numbers 6:1–4

In Numbers 6, God introduces the Nazirite vow. The word Nazirite means "one separated" or "one consecrated," so those who took this vow had a unique calling to live a certain way before God.

We read about several people in Scripture who took this vow and followed the rules God gave them to follow. One of them was Samson, whose story is familiar to many of us. An angel of the Lord appeared to his parents and told them they were going to have a son. The angel gave them instructions for Samson's life, saying, "For the child shall be a Nazirite to God from the womb" (Judg. 13:5).

We find another example of this calling in 1 Samuel 1:11: "And [Hannah] vowed a vow and said, 'O LORD of hosts, if you will indeed look on the affliction of your servant and remember me and not forget your servant, but will give to your servant a son, then I will give him to the LORD all the days of his life, and no razor shall touch his head.'" Hannah, who had been barren for many years, made a promise to God that if He gave her a child, she would give him back to God as one marked by the Nazirite vow.

These Nazirites were used by God to impact their generation and rescue people out of bondage. I believe that God is going to awaken Nazarites again—people who are set apart, who are in the world but not of it. If you want to reflect the image and the glory of God, you cannot be of this world. You need to be able to say to God, "I don't want to look like my friends. I don't want to look like my coworkers. Who cares that everyone allows alcohol or compromise—I want to be set apart so that Your glory can fill me."

Nazirites don't let any mixture in; they will never be lukewarm Christians. Why do you need alcohol when you have Jesus, who gives you waters to drink from that will make you never thirst again! The Nazarites set themselves apart before the cross; how much more are we able to separate ourselves by the power of the Holy Spirit? Let Jesus in you separate you from the world.

Everybody else might be okay with a little bit of alcohol, gossip, pornography, lust, cussing, stealing, or greed. But those who are consecrated have separated themselves unto God. Whether those things He calls you to give up are right or wrong in themselves does not matter. The call is to lay things down for Him, whatever He is asking of you, which is a beautiful offering to the Lord. God is awakening those who will go after Him with all their hearts.

That is what these generals of the faith did. They didn't settle for the easiest path. They were hungry for all that God had for their lives and were willing to give up anything to see His kingdom come.

THE FUTURE GENERALS

There are many generals of the faith we could talk about who understood the power of prayer—Catherine Booth, Smith Wigglesworth, A.W. Tozer, A.A. Allen, and T.L. Osborn, or even generals of our era like Corey Russell, Eric Gilmour, Mike Dow, Daniel Kolenda, Reinhard Bonnke, Andrew Barron, Steve Hill, and many more. But one thing that connects all these men and women is the fact that they had a deep prayer life. They were all in sync with God, and God was able to use them as vessels for His glory. In the

---

[8] Smith Wigglesworth, Smith Wigglesworth on Prayer, Power, and Miracles, comp. Roberts Liardon (Shippensburg, PA: Destiny Image, 2006), 78.

powerful words of Smith Wigglesworth, "It is as we feed on the Word and meditate on the message it contains, that the Spirit of God can vitalize that which we have received, and bring forth through us the word of knowledge that will be as full of power and life as when He, the Spirit of God, moved upon holy men of old and gave them these inspired Scriptures."[8]

God can use you too. As you grow your relationship with the Father, you will get in tune with what heaven has to say. Then you can be a useful vessel to bring heaven to earth. You too can be a general for the next generation.

MARK MOROZOV

FIVE
FASTING AND PRAYING

John Wesley was a man of God who started the Methodist movement in the eighteenth century. He was greatly used by God even in the face of great persecution and opposition—largely from those inside the church. There are many Methodist churches all over the world today because of what God did through that movement.

When Wesley would interview people for his staff, they were immediately disqualified if they weren't fasting for at least two days a week. Wesley had a lifestyle of fasting and praying, and he didn't want anyone on his team who was walking in the flesh and not in the Spirit.

Why was fasting so important to John Wesley? And why is it so important for us today? All kinds of people fast—Christians, Muslims, witch doctors, and many others. One of the five pillars of Islam is fasting. I remember sitting with a Muslim guy in Africa who was so hungry for the truth. How is it that Muslims have so much more zeal and passion in their fasting and prayer than we Christians do?

So what's the point of fasting as Christians? Is it just a religious practice that is no different from what Muslims do? Simply abstaining from food is not enough. You can fast all you want and not enter into the blessings God has for you—if you do it with a religious spirit.

Fasting is always attached to prayer. When we fast, we are seeking the face of God. As we do, we receive His power and revelation and are equipped for everything He has called us to accomplish. We will see strongholds torn down and captives set free. Fasting brings our flesh and our natural desires lower and exalts Christ to the highest place in our lives. Fasting brings our flesh and our natural desires lower and exalts Christ to the highest place in our lives.

But there's a problem in our generation: we don't fast. Many Christians don't understand the treasure and blessing of it. There are certainly some who fast and seek God in this way, but it's not as common as it should be. Why is fasting so rare in the church today? I believe it is for a few reasons. Firstly, we lack knowledge. Secondly, the enemy is constantly trying to oppose those who seek God through fasting and prayer. And thirdly, we give up too quickly.

The Bible says that God's people are destroyed because they

lack knowledge (Hosea 4:6). We do have some teaching on fasting, but I believe that you will never truly understand it until you try it. The deeper you go into fasting, the more you will understand what it is all about. The revelation you receive as you fast is so much more than you could ever be taught. Psalm 34:8 says, "Taste and see that the LORD is good!" If you want to understand fasting more, enter into it fully and see what God will do in and through you.

Michael Dow said, "Only the truly hungry will fast."[9] His book Fasting: Rediscovering the Ancient Pathways has opened my eyes so much to the blessings of fasting. And I know that Michael lives what he preaches. The reason he walks powerfully in the anointing is because he embraces a lifestyle of fasting and praying.

When you start fasting, everything will try to stop you from doing it. When you try to draw near to God, things will come along and attempt to distract you. Every time I fast, someone comes along and offers me free food—and usually the best kind of food! We have to stand our ground when these temptations come our way and let God do what He wants to do in us.

In order to fully benefit from fasting, you must sacrifice your own desires. It's difficult, especially in America where we see advertisements for delicious food everywhere! We have so much abundance here; we are blessed to live in a prosperous nation. But there's a sacrifice we need to bring to God in order to burn brighter for Him.

I mentioned that another reason fasting is so weak in the body of Christ is that people give up too easily. To keep a fire going, you have to keep adding wood to it. If you want to have the power and

---

[9] Michael Dow, Fasting: Rediscovering the Ancient Pathways (Orlando, FL: Burning Ones, 2016), https://www.amazon.com/Fasting-Rediscovering-Ancient-Michael-Dow/dp/098921852X.

anointing of God, to be filled with the fire of the Holy Spirit, you must continually add logs to the fire. One way we do this is through fasting and praying. This is true of the people we look up to who are on fire for God. They stay that way because they continue to fast and pray. And as they do, they receive more and more revelation of who God is, stirring up their hunger for Him.

> ***If you want to have the power and anointing of God, to be filled with the fire of the Holy Spirit, you must continually add logs to the fire.***

We need the power of the Holy Spirit in our days. Paul wrote, "My speech and my message were not in plausible words of wisdom, but in demonstration of the Spirit and of power" (1 Cor. 2:4), and, "For the kingdom of God does not consist in talk but in power" (1 Cor. 4:20). We see the kingdom of God operating in power in the lives of Jesus and His disciples. Why don't we see the same things today that we read about in the Bible? The Holy Spirit lives in us, so why are these things not happening? It's because there's a price you have to pay to walk in this power. Fasting is that price.

As you begin to fast and seek God, He will move through you by the power of the Holy Spirit. Fasting truly activates the power of God in your life. Fasting is the positioning of your heart and life to receive all that Jesus has for you. Yes, Jesus paid the price so that you don't have to. He freely gives abundant life to you, but why are you not seeing the fullness? Fasting helps unlock those things in your life. Fasting positions you to access what Jesus has for you.

When you fast, you always walk out with something. You might only see it at the end of your fast, but you will receive something.

One time, after I had just finished a seven-day fast, I was at a vision brunch meeting for another ministry, and I kept noticing someone looking at me. Eventually, this man came up to me and asked me to tell him about myself. He then said that God had told him to pray for me. As he prayed, he asked God for an impartation of dreams and visions for my life. I was filled with the Holy Spirit so powerfully as he prayed; I have never felt the presence of God through someone's prayer as I did at that moment.

I came home from that meeting and went to sleep. Sometime that night I woke up from a dream and went straight into a vision where God was speaking to me about His Word being a lamp to my feet and a light to my path. I kept seeing this vision for the next few weeks.

After another period of fasting, I began to see many more healings than I had before. You might not know what you will receive, but God knows what you need. There are things that God has for you if you will just seek Him in fasting and prayer.

FASTING AS A LIFESTYLE

Fasting is not merely an event; it's a lifestyle—at least it should be. As you enter in, you will see so much victory in your life. Sometimes we think that we can pray or fast once and then we'll be filled up and set for everything ahead. But it shouldn't stop there. It's not a one-off; it's a lifestyle of being filled up by God so that we overflow to those around us. Remember, those who diligently seek Him will be rewarded (Heb. 11:6).

> *"And Jesus said to them, 'Can the wedding guests fast while the bridegroom is with them? As long as they have the bridegroom with them, they cannot fast.'"*
> —Mark 2:19

Jesus was walking with His disciples when some people came up to Him asking why His disciples were not fasting when the Pharisees and the disciples of John the Baptist were. Jesus' response teaches us a lot. When the bridegroom is gone you need to fast, because when you fast, Jesus comes. When Jesus was with the disciples, they didn't need to fast because He was already there. But when He is gone, we need to fast so that He will come near to us. The devil doesn't want us fasting because he doesn't want us to get closer to Jesus.

> *"I appeal to you therefore, brothers, by the mercies of God, to present your bodies as a living sacrifice, holy and acceptable to God, which is your spiritual worship. 2 Do not be conformed to this world, but be transformed by the renewal of your mind, that by testing you may discern what is the will of God, what is good and acceptable and perfect."*
> —Romans 12:1–2

There's one place where your body becomes holy—in fasting. You begin to hunger for God, He reveals your sins, you receive revelation, and you become holy. The world tries to influence our minds and our understanding so that we will be like everybody else. But Jesus calls us to sacrifice ourselves fully to His kingdom and His ways.

But fasting is a sacrifice. Living the lifestyle God calls us to requires us to give up things that the world offers. We have so many resources at our disposal to use for the kingdom of God, but we're often happy to just enjoy life's pleasures and not seek God. The narrow path is the hard path, and the world won't understand it when you truly follow Jesus.

I've seen many people who had huge dreams about how they were going to serve God with their lives. Some wanted to go overseas as missionaries, and others wanted to start orphanages. But over time many of these dreams just disappeared. They were true desires from God, but the devil stole them away. Why? Because comfort set in. A natural conforming to the world began to set in.

When we are so worried about our own safety and security, we can forfeit the dreams of God because they seem too hard or risky. But we must remember that as long as we are pursuing Jesus, He will provide all that we need. He has so much more for each of us if we will just trust Him to provide the vision, clarity, people, funds, open doors, food, and more. I have never lacked provision while I have been in ministry. God has always provided, sometimes in the most unusual ways. I have never lacked people to support me or any opportunities. So if God calls you, obey.

If God calls you, obey.

FASTING AS SPIRITUAL WARFARE

"For the weapons of our warfare are not of the flesh but have divine power to destroy strongholds. 5 We destroy arguments and every lofty opinion raised against the knowledge of God, and take every thought captive to obey Christ, being ready to punish every disobedience, when your obedience is complete."
—2 Corinthians 10:4–6

The Bible talks often about spiritual battles. We have weapons that can pull down strongholds in the spiritual realm, things that are exalting themselves against Christ. Sometimes there are things in our lives that we place higher than Christ. It's important that we pull them down. Fasting helps us put God first and put everything else in place. It helps us put our priorities in order. Yes, food is good, but sometimes we need to sacrifice food in order to give Christ the highest place in our lives. Everything needs to go down, and Christ needs to go up.

There was a time when Elisha and his servant were surrounded by the Syrian army, who knew that Elisha was a powerful man of God and wanted to kill him. Elisha's servant was afraid when he saw the army surrounding the city, but Elisha said to him, "Do not be afraid, for those who are with us are more than those who are with them" (2 Kings 6:16). The passage continues: "Then Elisha prayed and said, 'O LORD, please open his eyes that he may see.' So the LORD opened the eyes of the young man, and he saw, and behold, the mountain was full of horses and chariots of fire all around Elisha" (2 Kings 6:17). The servant only saw the natural army, but the spiritual reality was opened up to him after Elijah prayed.

When we enter into fasting, we tap into the supernatural. God begins to reveal things to us about our lives and about the world around us. God created us to walk in the spirit, and our eyes are opened to true reality when we fast. The more you go into the place of fasting and praying, the more you will understand the things going on in your life. God wants us to understand His perspective, not just to believe what the circumstances look like around us or what everyone else is saying. The Bible talks about the will of the Father being done on earth as it is in heaven. There is a heavenly perspective and purpose waiting to be revealed through you on this earth.

There was a time when the disciples couldn't cast a demon out of a young boy, but when the boy was brought to Jesus, he was set free. The disciples asked Jesus why they had failed to cast the demon out, and Jesus said something very interesting:

"This kind can come out by nothing but prayer and fasting."
—Mark 9:29

"Because of your unbelief; for assuredly, I say to you, if you have faith as a mustard seed, you will say to this mountain, 'Move from here to there,' and it will move; and nothing will be impossible for you. 21 However, this kind does not go out except by prayer and fasting."
—Matthew 17:20–21

When you fast and pray, unbelief will leave and you will be able to heal the sick and cast out demons. It wasn't that the disciples had to work their way to gain authority—that's religion. They needed to fast to position themselves to use the authority Jesus freely gives.

They had to draw near to God so that their unbelief would be broken off and they could access the faith to take authority over demonic strongholds.

When we fast, we die to ourselves and receive Jesus' life. Some of you are plagued even generationally by doubts and you need to fast to break off these mindsets. Some things are received only by fasting and praying.

It wasn't that the disciples had to work their way to gain authority—that's religion.

"Fear not, Daniel, for from the first day that you set your heart to understand and humbled yourself before your God, your words have been heard, and I have come because of your words. 13 The prince of the kingdom of Persia withstood me twenty-one days, but Michael, one of the chief princes, came to help me, for I was left there with the kings of Persia, 14 and came to make you understand what is to happen to your people in the latter days. For the vision is for days yet to come."
—Daniel 10:12–14

Daniel fasted for twenty-one days and didn't give up. The angel didn't arrive in the middle of the fast but right at the end. There was a spiritual battle that hindered the angel from coming to Daniel at the beginning of his fast, but because of Daniel's consistency, Michael came to help with the battle and the angel was able to deliver the message to Daniel.

The spiritual battle is real, so make sure you persevere to the end according to what God has called you to do. If God calls you to fast for three days, go for three days. If He calls you for ten days, go for ten days. There is a reason He is calling you to fast that you might not even know at the time. Persevere in your fasting so that you can receive everything God has for you—right up until the end. Try to fast for nothing but Jesus. Let Jesus be the Lord of your fasting life. He knows what fast you need. If you fast, you will get what He has for you and what He wants for you. When you find Him, you get all that you need.

> *"But seek first the kingdom of God and his righteousness, and all these things will be added to you."*
> —Matthew 6:33

MARK MOROZOV

SIX
THREE TYPES OF PRAYER

There are many different types of prayers that we can talk about. I don't think this book can contain them all. Personally, I don't think there should be a formula for how to pray. As a matter of fact, as the disciples walked with Jesus and saw the fruit of His ministry, they realized the reason why Jesus had this fruit in His life was that He prayed differently. They went to Him and said, "Teach us to pray" (Luke 11:1).

I'm sure the disciples knew how to pray. They had watched Him, and they might have even repeated His prayers. But they wanted to find out what the difference was with Jesus. I think it's the same way with worship. You can know all the information about worship, and you can be around some of the best worshipers, but if you don't connect with worship yourself—if you don't really taste and see—then you won't really know the power of worship, or the power of prayer, or the power of the different ways that you can connect with the Father. I want to mention a few different types of prayer that have been a blessing for me. I believe they will be powerful instruments for you as well.

WORSHIP

The first type of prayer that I want to mention is worship. I truly believe worship is such a powerful tool that the Father has given us so we can connect with heaven and hear what heaven has to say. The devil is after our hearing. He doesn't want us to hear what heaven is saying. He wants to block our ears from hearing the Father so that we never bring heaven down on earth. But there is such a powerful key in releasing heaven's worship on earth.

Before I really knew Jesus, I was living in bondage, addiction, and sin. I remember turning on a Christian radio station while driving my work truck even though I wasn't a Christian, didn't go to church, and was living in sin. I knew about the Lord, but at the time I was running away from Him. But I would drive and turn on 88.1—a Christian station in my city. As I listened to the worship that was playing, I would get so full of the Holy Spirit. I would get consumed by Jesus even though a few minutes earlier I had been listening to songs filled with cussing. Day to day I would have more of a desire to experience the presence of God that I felt while listening to that worship music. I wanted to connect with heaven more.

Each time I turned the Christian station on, I would get filled with God's glory, and it got to the point where I decided I wanted to attend a church service. That was the moment I gave my life to Jesus. But it didn't start at the service for me; it started when I turned on worship in my car, even though I wasn't living for Jesus. There is such power in worship. It wasn't a prayer meeting that drew me in or a church service or conference that initially sparked my love for the Lord. It was worship.

It wasn't a prayer meeting that drew me in, or a church service or conference that initially sparked my love for the Lord. It was worship.

I've mentioned this already, but if you're not hungry for Jesus but you decide to connect with heaven and receive in worship or prayer, you will find yourself wanting more of Jesus. Jesus is the bread that does not end. He's the waters that do not run dry. And He's the One who can make rivers in the wastelands. If it seems like God might be far away from you and there's a drought, just come and drink a little bit. That's what happened to me in worship. He gave me a little bit of salt on the edge of my tongue. Salt makes you more thirsty. He let me taste and see that He is good. And that's what caused me to thirst for more of Him.

Sometimes we don't feel the Lord's presence, so we stop coming to Him. But listen—we show up to Him, for Him. Not for a certain feeling, because we walk by faith and not by sight. So just keep coming. Many times the breakthrough is just around the corner, but we give up too early.

Many times when people tell me they don't have time to worship or pray, their lifestyle doesn't agree with this. They sit on social media for six hours, hang out with friends for three hours, watch the news for another two hours, and then they have no time for Jesus. They have time, they're just not prioritizing Him. There are other gods in their lives besides Jesus.

The Lord desires for us to connect with heaven, and one of the ways to connect with heaven is through worship. I've seen myself connect with heaven through worship more than any other way.

When the disciples asked Jesus how to pray, He started by saying, "Our Father in heaven, hallowed be your name" (Matt. 6:9). Jesus started with praise. And so should we. We begin with worship, lifting up the name of Jesus, and as we connect to Him, we can then flow in prayer. I've noticed that when I feel like my prayer life is stale, all I do is start worshiping until there's a breakthrough.

COSTLY WORSHIP

I hear a lot of controversy and attacks against charismatic Christians for being a little wild in worship. But a lot of these believers are just free. They're free from the fear of man. They're free from the pressure to perform. People can learn the outward language of Christianity, even of worship, but not be truly connected with heaven. Yes, there are people whose outward expression is just a performance rather than a true expression of their heart. But I would prefer to see them at least trying rather than giving up and just standing there like a dead corpse. It's always the dead ones that have something to say against the ones breaking the flask and pouring their sacrifice unto the Lord.

> ***People can learn the outward language of Christianity, even of worship, but not be truly connected with heaven.***

The Father is looking for people who will worship Him in spirit and in truth (John 4:24). He's looking for worship. True worship is when you're worshiping from your heart, in the Spirit, and in truth. It's not just imitating a group of people who are all doing the same thing. I would prefer to see them at least trying rather than giving up and just standing there like a dead corpse.

Worship will cost you. Sometimes it's not going to look normal—if you're willing to become a true worshiper, you will be criticized at times. David danced before the Lord, and his wife criticized him, but it was true worship before God. It was how David connected with heaven. You can be standing still but your heart is connecting with Him. Or you can be moving around with your heart connected with Him. It doesn't matter.

We're too worried about what everybody else thinks. We get so worried about how our worship looks that we end up worshiping worry rather than the Father. We're worshiping fear of man—what somebody else thinks or what somebody else has to say. We can even end up worshiping "worship" when we're too distracted by what everybody else thinks.

I once spoke with a leader who told me he gave all his singers microphones with wires to make sure they didn't move around too much and attract attention to themselves. It sounded like putting a leash on a dog! You're containing the worship and the flow. You're containing somebody else's worship. We need to teach people not to worry about how the leaders are worshiping because we are worshiping Jesus, not them. I walk into so many places where the people are worshiping the worship leaders. Everyone's just standing there like a religious ceremony. Jesus is not dead; He is alive and living!

The worshipers should be connected to Jesus and connect others to Jesus. When we worship, the King is in the room. Who cares what other people's worship looks like? Do not worry about what everybody else is saying and the way everyone else is worshiping. If someone else's worship is distracting you, then I would question, who are you worshiping?

Instead of restricting how people worship, I think we need to teach people to continuously redirect their gaze to the Father. The Father will tone them down if needed. The New Covenant is a personal covenant. No priest is needed. We are the priests and can hear Him for ourselves. Yes, we need spiritual leaders who can help us. But there is a difference between help and control.

Too many leaders want to control. Be careful not to lead with control—we must give all control to Jesus. Allow Jesus to decide what needs to take place. We say God is a God of order, but who decides what order is—us or Jesus? The beauty of Jesus is that His love is not forceful. Jesus did not perform many miracles in His hometown because the people did not want it. Those that did, got it. If we place restrictions on Him, He will not force Himself on us. The Father is a gentleman and will honor the measure that we give Him. He will move in the measure in which we allow Him to move.

Give Jesus 100 percent today. Lean into Jesus and connect with Him on a personal level. We can only connect people to a Jesus we know. Connect others to Jesus, not to a golden calf we say is Jesus. That's what Paul was doing when he wrote his letters to the

New Testament churches—he was refocusing the gaze of the church back on Jesus. Many of them were losing focus, getting mixed up, and losing the truth—even though they knew it and had believed it before.

Worship God. Who cares what's happening on the outside? If everyone is standing still but you're moving and worshiping with your hands raised, you'd better not worry about what anyone else thinks because the moment you start worrying, it's going to rob you of the chance to fully worship God. If you're leading others in worship, make sure that you have your own flow with God. Make sure that you are connected with Him—not on the outside, but on the inside.

I can recognize an anointed worshiper not because of how beautifully they sing but because of the glory on their life. This is available not just for them but also for you. Everyone I know who flows in the glory has spent a great amount of personal time with the Lord. They take people where they have already been. You cannot take someone somewhere you have not been yourself. When you have been with Jesus, you can lead people to Him. You don't lead people to your set list or your formula; you take people to Him by hearing what heaven has to say as you're connected with Jesus.

> ***When you have been with Jesus, you are able to lead people to Him.***

The world longs for the revealing of the sons of God. Why? Because true sons know their Father. Sons break the curse off of humanity. But those who live as orphans, even though they still have a Father, they do not know Him. When you know the Father, you become a dwelling place for His glory—where you go, His glory also goes. And His glory flows through you and breaks the curse off of humanity. It shifts atmospheres in workplaces and even regions, like we read about with Charles Finney.

If you don't have your own worship life or prayer life, then it will be hard for you to have a strong relationship with the Father. How will you know what the Father sounds like? How will you know if you're connected to the Father or not?

Too many people are worried about connecting to the wrong source instead of focusing on connecting to the Father. If you're connected to the Father, you don't need to worry about other sources. We worry about all these other spirits but don't even know God. I question whether those motives are God-based or fear-based.

When you know God, when you're connected with God, when you have a relationship with God, when you're worshiping the Father, then you don't need to worry about being deceived, because you know His voice. Sheep know the Shepherd's voice, and they do not follow another (John 10:27).

SACRIFICE OF WORSHIP

Biblical faith has a physical expression. Your life will show what you actually believe. And there's a price to pay for true worship. You have to die to all other gods. You have to die to the fear of man, worshiping leaders, worshiping worship leaders, worshiping your job or career, worshiping your finances, worshiping your addiction or your depression. We tend to worship things that we place higher than God.

That's why I love true worship: it puts God back at the top. Then all the other patterns we have created and the things we created from our religious habits fall away. Yes, we can cause ourselves to worship patterns. We can cause ourselves to worship our way of doing things rather than God Himself. We can worship our setlist. If this is you, I am thankful this book is in your hands. From this moment on, this will no longer be the category you are in.

Paul tells us to pray without ceasing (1 Thess. 5:17). It's a constant connection—an awareness of God. If you're constantly aware of God wherever you are, He can use you as His vessel—in your career, business, or ministry. Ministry isn't just for those on the stage singing or preaching; it's everywhere you go as you minister to Him.

> *"And while he was at Bethany in the house of Simon the leper, as he was reclining at table, a woman came with an alabaster flask of ointment of pure nard, very costly, and she broke the flask and poured it over his head."*
> *—Mark 14:3*

The woman in this story (we find out in John's Gospel that it is Mary of Bethany) understood this lifestyle of worship. She gave herself fully to Jesus, even though it looked foolish to those around her as she broke an expensive flask of perfume and poured it all on Jesus. Her worship looked like sacrifice, and it released a sweet aroma. Sacrifice always releases an aroma to heaven.

What sacrifice do you need to make today? Maybe it is to sacrifice the fear of man. Maybe you need to sacrifice financial security. Do you love finances more than you love God? Do you love your security more than you love God? Maybe you love pleasing people more than pleasing God. What is God asking you to lay down so that you can release more worship? Sometimes we have a stale worship life because we've allowed these higher things in our lives to rob us of our connection with heaven.

What is God asking you to lay down so that you can release more worship?

Do you come out of your prayer time and realize it was really stale? Maybe it's because the whole prayer time has been about you. You've been worshiping yourself in the prayer time, or you've been worshiping the prayer time itself. Or you've been worshiping your depression. "God, why am I depressed?" Go in there and worship Jesus. Don't worship worship itself. Let Him be the Lord of your worship time. Say, "God, help me. Lead me in this worship moment."

NEHEMIAH

There's a story in Nehemiah chapter 13, the last chapter, that many people miss because it seems like the story has finished. But what was going on after Nehemiah finished building the walls of Jerusalem? There was a revival! But when Nehemiah returned to Jerusalem after some time away, there was no more revival.
There was just staleness. What happened?

"Now before this, Eliashib the priest, who was appointed over the chambers of the house of our God, and who was related to Tobiah, 5 prepared for Tobiah a large chamber where they had previously put the grain offering, the frankincense, the vessels, and the tithes of grain, wine, and oil, which were given by commandment to the Levites, singers, and gatekeepers, and the contributions for the priests."
—Nehemiah 13:4–5

In the city, there was a storehouse where people would bring their sacrifices and worship God. There was continuous worship and continuous revival. But when Nehemiah came back, he realized that the priest had put Tobiah in the storehouse, so the people stopped bringing their sacrifices. The sacrifices stopped, which caused the worship to stop, which stopped the revival. People could not bring sacrifices; therefore, they could not release worship.

Who was this Tobiah? He was the one who was trying to stop Nehemiah from building the walls at the beginning. He was the one trying to stop Nehemiah from fulfilling the call of God. Worship was replaced with sin. The priest replaced worshiping God with the man he was probably worried about.

I can imagine the lies Tobiah must have told the priest. He might have said, "Hey, I need a place to stay. Don't leave me outside with nowhere to live. You have a whole storehouse! Put me in there. I need somewhere to sleep." I think Eliashib gave in to the fear of man. The result was that all the priests and Levites left the ministry. They all stopped serving God.

Why? Because the offerings would also pay the priests to continue in their ministry. And the offerings paid the Levites to keep worshiping. They had full-time worshipers who weren't getting paid anymore so they had to leave their ministry to earn money in some other occupation.

Too often we find Tobiah in the storehouse of the body of Christ today. God wants to clean the house. He wants to restore worship. What is the Tobiah in your life? Is it the fear of man? Is it worrying about what everyone else thinks more than what God thinks? Is it your greed in your finances? Have you allowed success to take hold of you so deeply that it has robbed you of your worship? Do you have a relationship in your life that has stolen the place God is supposed to possess? Are you so worried about everything in life that it's robbing you of worship? The Lord wants to clean the house of your life, and He wants to clean the house of the body of Christ. He wants to remove every sin and every high thing that exalts itself above the name of Jesus, to restore true worship, to restore revival, to restore the move of God.

When Nehemiah returned, he kicked the priest out and removed Tobiah, and then the worship began to flow again. Revival came back to the people. It is time to clean house so that worship can come back to the house of God. Everyone wants revival, but we want it on our terms. Revival will only flow on His terms. Will you clean house and submit to His ways, to allow the revival to flow into our generation through you?

It is time to clean house so that worship can come back to the house of God.

FIGHTING THROUGH WORSHIP

You know, some battles are only won in worship. My old youth pastor would often write worship as "war-ship." We understood that worship is a time of fighting. It's a time of gaining victory. The Bible says in the Book of Ephesians that our fight is not against flesh and blood but against spiritual principalities (Eph. 6:12). So if our fight is spiritual, there's only one way to fight it: spiritually! And one of the ways to fight our battles is through worship.

How do we fight our battles with worship? Well, for one, we already have victory through Jesus, so we don't even need to fight. We can let Jesus fight for us. We just worship Him because it's already done; it's already finished. We worship out of the place of victory. You praise Him, and it manifests the victory.

Worship causes you to see victory, breakthroughs, and the answers in your life. I believe there's nothing like worship to the Lord. He loves it; He enjoys it. As a matter of fact, we will be worshiping in heaven more than anything else. Everyone's sitting around the throne, saying "Holy, holy, holy" for all of eternity. Some words get old for us, but they never get old for God. We will want to worship Him even more.

JEHOSHAPHAT

We see this "war-ship" demonstrated with King Jehoshaphat in 2 Chronicles 20. The people were going into battle, but they were outnumbered by the enemy. Did they try to come up with their own strategy? Did they consult the people? Or did they go to God? King Jehoshaphat ran straight to the Father and said, "What do I do, Lord? I don't know what to do."

The Lord gave Jehoshaphat instructions. He told him to put the worshipers on the front lines with their worship instruments. Jehoshaphat did what God told him to do. He set up his worship leaders with their instruments on the front lines, and they went into battle, worshiping. The Bible says that their enemies ended up turning against each other and killing one another. By the time Jehoshaphat got to the place where the enemies were, they were all wiped out. The people of God walked out with great spoils. Not only did God give them victory in the battle, but He also gave them blessings after the battle.

That's what worship does. When problems come, we should not run to people; we should run to Jesus. You can just worship because the victory has been won on the cross and we get to tap into it through worship. When you worship, you will always walk out with something. You always walk out with more of God. With more joy, more breakthroughs, and more peace. When you understand this, it helps you worship.

WAITING

How can I talk about prayer and not mention the story of Mary? This is such a powerful story. The Bible even says that wherever the Gospel is preached, the story of Mary will be told (Mark 14:9). Mary is mentioned several times in the Bible, and I want to connect her story with the second type of prayer: waiting on the Lord.

> *"Now as they went on their way, Jesus entered a village. And a woman named Martha welcomed him into her house. 39 And she had a sister called Mary, who sat at the Lord's feet and listened to his teaching. 40 But Martha was distracted with much serving. And she went up to him and said, 'Lord, do you not care that my sister has left me to serve alone? Tell her then to help me.' 41 But the Lord answered her, 'Martha, Martha, you are anxious and troubled about many things, 42 but one thing is necessary. Mary has chosen the good portion, which will not be taken away from her.'"*
> —Luke 10:38–42

Sometimes we're like Martha—we run around and try to do all sorts of things. Martha was running around trying to do a lot, but Mary was just sitting at the feet of Jesus. Martha tried to rebuke Mary and asked Jesus to tell her to do some work. You know those times when you're not doing what everybody else expects you to do, and everybody else tries to pressure you to do what they are doing? In their eyes, what they're doing is right.

But we always have to remember that Jesus shows us what is right. Obviously, it looks like Martha is doing great things. She's cooking, she's cleaning, she's preparing, and she's about to feed Jesus. But Jesus says, "Martha, what are you doing? Mary chose the right thing." Mary had chosen to sit at His feet and look at Him. She chose to look at His beauty, look at the way He breathed, look at the way He blinked, look at the way He sat. She watched Him so that she could get every glimpse of His face.

Martha was too busy trying to serve Jesus rather than to see Him. This is the problem with many people in the body of Christ. They need to stop what they're doing and look. We can get so busy with running and doing that we forget about looking at Jesus. That's what Jesus is after. He wants us to have a relationship with Him. That's what separates us from every other religion. Jesus is real and alive. He is on the throne today.

Jesus is real and alive. He is on the throne today.

In Revelation, Jesus tells the church in Ephesus that they have done everything right, but He has one thing against them: they lost their first love. They were like Martha, doing everything right and serving Jesus, but they had lost their first love for Him. Jesus tells them to repent and go back to that first love.

Mary chose the right thing. The Gospel is about having a relationship with Jesus. The Gospel says that even though you've forsaken Him, even though you've sinned, even though you've fallen short of His glory, He's here with arms wide open ready to love on you. He's ready for you to just sit with Him, to be with Him.

Sometimes waiting can feel like a waste of time. I've had many times where I've been in such a hurry to accomplish things that I feel like waiting won't achieve anything. But so much gets done in the waiting.

When you hold a baby, the baby might not say anything or do anything, but there is a spiritual and emotional connection. This is what happens when you're sitting with the Father. It might not feel like anything is happening, but there is a connection. There's an impartation happening and an opportunity to hear from God in the waiting that doesn't happen any other way.

I remember a time when I had an intercession room where I would pray all my lists off, praying for every single person in the name of Jesus, casting out devils from people on my list, and praying for my future. Once I remember walking out of my house after an hour of prayer, sitting in my car, and the Holy Spirit stopping me just as I turned on my car and saying, "What about Me?" I was so busy interceding that I had missed the Lord.

Sometimes waiting is exactly the right thing to do. When you wait on the Lord, you will receive breakthrough, freedom, and answers to your prayers. Even when it feels like nothing is happening, it's like a blade is being sharpened.

So many people feel like they have nothing to pray about, so they don't show up. Instead, just show up and wait, and I guarantee a sharpening will take place. The person you hang out with is the one you become like. When you spend time with Jesus—not necessarily saying or doing anything but just sitting there, waiting on Him, connecting with Him—you are being sharpened. Things shift. You're going to come out of there like Moses, reflecting the glory of God, shining like Jesus when He walked out from being with the Father. He was transfigured. You'll walk out of these times with God transfigured. You'll walk out looking more like Him.

That's what Jesus is looking for. He doesn't need our service. He needs our hearts. So many are after His hand but they miss His heart. And He wants our hearts more than our hands. He welcomes our hands, but He wants our hearts. This reality sets us free from so much expectation and exhausting religious activity. If you never serve a day in your life but you love Him, you are more successful than any person who will spend their whole life serving Him without ever knowing Him. The world needs those who truly know their Father. Wherever they show up, He shows up with them.

When you're saturated with the Lord, full of His glory from being with Him and waiting on Him, you can go into a place and change the atmosphere without even saying a word. You just show up and people experience breakthrough, freedom, and liberty. If the Lord shows up, devils leave.

Sometimes people feel like they need to pray for an hour to see healing. But when you are beholding the Lord, you just need to show up and He will do the healing. You don't need to be doing the talking when He does the healing. And when you show up, you bring everyone a new revelation of the Father. That's why the world needs you. That's why the world needs a revelation of the sons of God—because they carry a revelation of the Father. Why? Because they've spent time with Him. They've sat and they've watched Him.

There is so much teaching about Jesus, and everybody has their own opinion of what Jesus looks like, how He talks, and how He walks. But really there's only one place where you will find Him for yourself: when you wait for the Lord, He will be revealed.

I can remember many times when I didn't have any words to pray, so I just sat there. My only prayer was, "God, I need You." But I still showed up. And you know what? Every time I showed up, He showed up. Before preaching, services, and events, I just show up. I have few words, but I say, "God, You know my heart; You know my words. You know what I need." And He always comes through. Maybe you have no words. Just show up and wait. There's still something happening. God is still doing something in the background.

Every time I showed up, He showed up.

INTERCESSION

The final type of prayer I want to talk about is intercession. I remember one time when a woman of God came to the Bible school I was a part of and taught about putting on the full armor of God. She spoke about how we are warriors on the front lines and that the

Bible calls us to put on the armor of God so that when the day of evil comes, we will be able to withstand it.

So many believers wait to put on the armor until it's too late—when problems occur—but we need to put on our armor and get ready beforehand. The Bible says that God is looking for those who will stand in the gap for their generation (Ezek. 22:30). Often we wait until it's too late, but Jesus is offering us an invitation to stand in the gap now. After hearing this woman teach about the armor of God, I started to put on my armor in the Spirit as I prayed. I've seen a tremendous turnaround in my life and other people's lives through intercession.

There's something special about interceding for somebody else. So many times when you pray for somebody else, God comes through and answers your own prayers. I've seen in church services where a person would pray for somebody else to be healed, forgetting that they themselves had pain. But as they prayed for someone in pain at the altar, the Lord healed them and the other person at the same time.

> *"Therefore take up the whole armor of God, that you may be able to withstand in the evil day."*
> *—Ephesians 6:13*

The day of evil will come for everybody. Jesus knew it. You'll walk through different seasons of life, but Jesus says, "Fear not; I have overcome everything, and I'll help you overcome everything." (See John 16:33.) Jesus will walk with us, helping us overcome every challenge that the enemy throws at us. We have nothing to worry about if the Lord is on our side.

I believe intercession is the place where we can really stand in the gap and fight our battles. It's through intercession that we can take our families back, take our breakthrough back, take our freedom back, take our relationship with the Lord back, take our churches back, and take our generation back to our first love.

As I mentioned before, this fight is not against flesh and blood but against spiritual principalities. You see, it's a spiritual war. Some of you need to stand in the gap for your families. You've been waiting and you've tried to worship, but neither of those things have worked. You must begin to stand firm against the enemy.

I love the movie War Room. I remember the lady who was interceding. She stepped out, rebuked the devil, and told him to leave her family. She threw things outside and told the enemy that he didn't belong there. She was standing in the gap. She was interceding for her family.

There's so much power in that. There's such power in intercession. In intercession, we declare the Word of God over our situations. Even though you might feel forsaken, you declare what the Word says. "God, I thank You. You'll never forsake me." Even if you don't always feel God in your prayer life, say to Him, "God, I thank You that You'll never leave me or forsake me. You're always with me." Even if you aren't seeing a breakthrough in your finances, say, "God, I thank You that You're going to bless me. You're going to make rivers in the wasteland." If you feel like God is far away, you can declare that the Word says you will prosper. You'll be the head and not the tail.

I've seen God show up as I interceded. I remember one time when I had it on my heart to pray for my cousin. She wasn't really strong in her relationship with the Lord. As I was interceding for her, I said, "God, I thank You. She will go to Bible school, she will learn from You, and she will know You." I felt such authority in the Spirit as I released those words. All of a sudden at the end of the prayer I started thanking God that not only was she going to Bible school but also all her tuition was going to be paid for.

About thirty minutes after I finished praying, I got a phone call. It was my cousin. I want you to understand that we didn't hang out all the time. We weren't that close to where she would call me. What are the odds? She said to me, "Hey, I have some good news to tell you. I'm going to Bible school. And not only am I going to Bible school, but I have even better news. I'm going to Bible school with somebody, and they said they'll cover my whole tuition."

I was so amazed! I asked her, "What made you call me?"
She said, "I don't know. I just felt like I had to call you and tell you." I told her that I had just been interceding for her, praying for her to go to Bible school and praying for her to get her whole tuition covered. And that's exactly what happened! I could share a whole book of testimonies like this, but unfortunately, we are limited to what needs to be shared in the short remainder of this book. The time to intercede is now.

There is such power in intercession. There's such power in standing in the gap. You are a warrior. Take back what is rightfully yours. Do not let the devil win. Do not let the devil take what's yours. Fight this battle in the spirit. Jesus has given you the authority. You have rights as an ambassador, as a son or daughter of God. Jesus took the keys from the devil and gave them freely to you. Now go and take back what's yours!

Jesus took the keys from the devil and gave them freely to you. Now go and take back what's yours!

SEVEN
CALL TO ACTION

Many people do not pray because they don't know what prayer is. People do not pray because they don't understand why they need to pray. People truly do not pray because they do not truly love God. If you love someone, you want to spend time with them. It's not necessarily the person's fault that they don't pray or don't know that they need to pray. Many times it's just a lack of knowledge. Spend time with Jesus today and watch how quickly you will fall in love with Him.

Today's American gospel says, "Pray the prayer and you're going to heaven." But the true Gospel is more of an invitation to lay down your life and follow after God. Sometimes people don't pray because they know that after they've prayed, the Lord might call them to lay something down. The Lord might call them to go forgive somebody, give financially to somebody, or start fasting. We often don't want to do these things, so we stay away from true communion with the Father. Our flesh doesn't like it, but our flesh has to die. The Lord calls us to deny ourselves, pick up our cross, and follow Him. It takes death to the flesh to continue to follow Him.

A pastor once told me about a horrific dream he had. In this dream, he was eating steak. He was cutting different pieces of meat, which were cooked perfectly. (This pastor loves steak very much, and I believe that's why the Lord spoke to him in this way.) He took a piece with his fork and brought it to his mouth, but as he brought it closer, the piece of meat began to turn into flesh—and then it turned into a living rat. The rat began to run from the fork onto his hand. He flung it off his hand, completely disgusted.

When the pastor woke up from the dream with this feeling of disgust, the Lord spoke to him. He said, "Just like that, nobody will like to eat anything that is still alive. People only eat dead things. People only eat dead meats, cooked meat. People do not eat living flesh, living meat. In the same way, people will only receive from you when you are dead, when it's no longer you who lives, but Christ who lives in you. People will only receive from Jesus."

People do not need you; they need Jesus in you. And it's time for you to allow Jesus to shine from within you, wherever you are: at your job, your school or workplace, your business, and even your Ministry.

People do not need you; they need Jesus in you.

So many people today burn out from pursuing Jesus. If there was anyone who had it rough, it was Jesus. If there was anyone who could have called it quits, it was Jesus. Think about the Garden of Gethsemane, where it seemed like His impending death was just too much for Him to bear. Still, Jesus never burnt out. There is a way of life where you never burn out, where you continue to shine and impact people's lives even when you are not saying anything but just living your life, radiating Jesus.

Jesus did not burn out because He was always in sync with His Father. He only did what the Father told Him to do. The Father knows how to help you not to burn out. He knows how to sustain you. He can help you be blessed, successful, prosperous, and victorious, and to conquer everything that tries to entangle you and slow you down.

The enemy wants to take you away from prayer so that you begin to do everything in your own strength. You can still do a lot of things, but they're going to amount to nothing. It will be pointless because it's going to be you doing them, not God. So today, let Him do it through you. Let Him do it in you. Let Him do it around you.

Sometimes the best thing you can tell someone is no. This can be very spiritual, so spiritual that you may lose things like friends, jobs, and ministry opportunities. If the devil cannot stop you, he will push you to go faster so that you miss Jesus and do things without Him.

I've heard different leaders talk about people burning out in ministry. Some people will be on fire for Jesus and doing all these amazing things, but a year later they're done. They're burnt out; they're finished. They can't serve anymore, they can't lead anymore, they can't radiate Jesus anymore. Why? Because they never did it with Him. They might have started with Him, but at some point, they continued without Him. Eventually, their tank ran out. The battery ended up dying because they were not recharging it.

As we mentioned at the beginning of the book, serving Jesus without having a relationship with Him is lawlessness. The law kills, but the Spirit gives life. If you stay plugged in, your power source will never run dry. Your batteries will remain fully charged. If you continuously keep coming back to fuel up on gas, your car will continue to drive.

Many people try to fulfill their ministry calling without God and find themselves burnt out, tired, offended, discouraged, worried, and exhausted. Jesus did not burn out because He only did what the Father told Him to do. The disciples did not burn out and actually died for Jesus because they only did what the Father told them to do. Following the Father will protect you and cause you to do everything God put you on this earth to do.

The cure for all of this is to be full of oil. The cure for discouragement is to be full of oil. The cure for worry is to be full of oil. Oil will slip those things out of your life, and they will no longer have access to you.

Pastors, mentors, businessmen, and leaders: Do you want your leaders to continue to burn for Jesus? Connect them to Jesus. With all love, I say this humbly: Disciple makers, you must stop connecting disciples to yourself. Connect them to the Father. Businessmen, do you want to have success in your business? Connect your employees to the Father. Do you want to see fruit? Connect to the Source, not to the ministry.

KING ASA

At the beginning of his reign, King Asa "did what was good and right in the eyes of the LORD his God" (2 Chron. 14:2). Asa had learned from the mistakes of his father. He removed altars of foreign gods, removed the high places, broke down sacred pillars, and cut down wooden images. He commanded Judah to seek the Lord God of their fathers and to observe the law.

Asa had read the books and saw that when King David destroyed the idols and the kingdom was focused on God, it was prosperous. So he decided to do things like his forefather David had done them. He started building fortified cities in Judah. As he did these two things—tearing down idols and building cities—his enemies came against him.

Just because you're with the Lord doesn't mean everything is always going to be perfect. There will be battles that come your way—but fear not. Remember: God is with you. God is on your side. He will take you through the battle.

As war broke out, King Asa ran straight to God and cried out, "O LORD, there is none like you to help, between the mighty and the weak. Help us, O LORD our God, for we rely on you, and in your name we have come against this multitude. O LORD, you are our God; let not man prevail against you" (2 Chron. 14:11).

God told him, "I've got this battle. I'm going to help you with it." So the Lord struck down the Ethiopians before him. God gave him victory. And they carried away many spoils from the battle. Even though the enemy came against them, they were the ones who came out with the silver and gold.

You always come out on top when the devil tries to attack you. When you understand this and the devil tries to bring something against you, you're able to walk through it easily. God makes rivers in the wasteland (Isa. 43:19, NLT). You can laugh at the enemy because you know God is going to turn it all around.

So God turned it all around for King Asa. Then we read in chapter 15, "Hear me, Asa, and all Judah and Benjamin: The LORD is with you while you are with him. If you seek him, he will be found by you, but if you forsake him, he will forsake you" (2 Chron. 15:2). Basically, the prophet rebukes Asa. That's sharp! Asa has just won the war and come away with all the spoils, and now this prophet comes along and rebukes him. Why would he do that?

If you read a little lower, in verse 5, it says, "In those times there was no peace to him who went out or to him who came in, for great disturbances afflicted all the inhabitants of the lands." There was chaos and distress going on; everyone was affected. "But you, take courage! Do not let your hands be weak, for your work shall be rewarded" (v. 7).

What was King Asa's response to this prophecy? "As soon as Asa heard these words, the prophecy of Azariah the son of Oded, he took courage and put away the detestable idols" (v. 8).

Do you remember what happened at the beginning of Asa's reign? "He took away the foreign altars and the high places and broke down the pillars and cut down the Asherim" (2 Chron. 14:3). So if Asa already destroyed these pagan gods, and now it says he is destroying them again, where did they come from? They got built up again. Do you know how they got built up again? It was when God gave him much spoil. When his people carried away the spoils of war, there were foreign gods in this treasure. The blessing ended up being a curse.

We see this happen to a lot of successful businessmen, ministers, ministries, and churches. They start off strong, going after God. And God blesses them. But all of a sudden, corruption, envy, jealousy, sin, and many other things start rising. Then the enemy tries to make things from the past resurface—old ways of thinking that they had torn down. The only way forward is to let them die again.

Remember what we were talking about in Colossians? Paul said, "As you received Christ Jesus the Lord, so walk in him" (Col. 2:6). Don't just receive Him. Stay in Him—stay connected. When the body of Christ allows compromise, we slowly start to worship paganism. Paul was trying to direct the Colossians away from religion and to the true worship of God.

So here the prophet came and rebuked King Asa. His response was to take courage and obey the word of the Lord. It takes courage to tear down idols. It takes courage to say no to temptation. It takes courage to say no to what everybody else is doing. And Asa took courage. As a matter of fact, he took courage to such an extent that it says, "And they entered into a covenant to seek the LORD, the God of their fathers, with all their heart and with all their soul, but that whoever would not seek the LORD, the God of Israel, should be put to death, whether young or old, man or woman" (2 Chron. 15:12–13). Asa even removed his mother from being queen mother because of her idolatry.

Asa commanded everybody to seek God. He thought, That's it! We're not doing this again. I'm not having this again. This time we're going to worship God. We're going to destroy all these idols. And do you know what happened? "There was no more war until the thirty-fifth year of the reign of Asa" (v. 19). So things became peaceful again in Asa's kingdom. But fast-forward a few verses and another prophet comes with a message for the king. This time it was Hanani the seer who spoke to Asa:

> *"Because you relied on the king of Syria, and did not rely on the LORD your God, the army of the king of Syria has escaped you.[8] Were not the Ethiopians and the Libyans a huge army with very many chariots and horsemen? Yet because you relied on the LORD, he gave them into your hand.[9] For the eyes of the LORD run to and fro throughout the whole earth, to give strong support to those whose heart is blameless toward him. You have done foolishly in this, for from now on you will have wars."*
> —2 Chronicles 16:7–9

It then says that Asa was angry with Hanani and put him in prison. He also began oppressing the people at that time.

So here is King Asa, a man of God who was strong in the Lord, took action at the word of God, and cleansed his nation from idolatry, but later on in his life he didn't respond to God in the same way. Asa obeyed the word of the Lord through the first prophet but threw the second prophet in prison.

Some people begin on fire for the Lord. They're ready to do anything for Him. They destroy all the idols in their churches and submit to the work of the Holy Spirit. But later on in their lives, they're the very ones who are persecuting the next move of God.

We have seen this pattern repeat throughout the generations, and if you study revival, you will see it as well. How did King Asa end up like this? Why did King Solomon end his reign badly? Why do these failures keep repeating themselves? History repeats itself, and there is a slow turning away from God.

That is where we're headed as a nation right now. America is turning away from God, and the body of Christ needs to step up and cleanse itself, removing compromise, drinking, insecurities, competition, jealousy, and greed. Only then can God fill us again.

You're not going to be popular if you call out the sin that you see—the elephant in the room that nobody wants to talk about. But if you're worried about what people think, you're not concerned with what God is saying. He wants His house clean. The only way to get rid of the darkness is to turn on the light. Many have kept it off for too long. I will tell you something—this generation sees it and is tired of it.

A light is coming to this generation. They will not bow to any woke movement. They will bow to only one name: JESUS! Jesus gave His life for us that He may enter our hearts and enable us to finish until the end. His Holy Spirit will give us the power to deny the wrong voices and follow the right voice. He is our Shepherd, and we will not follow the voice of another. God gave His Holy Spirit to help us because He knew we could not make it without Him. We cannot seek the Father without His Spirit crying out, "Abba Father," drawing us to Him.

> ***A light is coming to this generation. They will not bow to any woke movement. They will bow to only one name: JESUS!***

King Asa started strong but finished poorly because he stopped running to the Father. May we finish stronger than we started. The moment we hear a word from the Lord, even a rebuke, let's get on our faces before Him, saying, "God, I'm going to stick with You no matter what. I've noticed I've been in sin too much, working too much, angry too much, ministering too much. I've been doing too much, and I haven't been with You." If we humble ourselves before the Lord, He will give us the grace to finish well.

If we humble ourselves before the Lord, He will give us the grace to finish well.

KEEPING THE END IN MIND

It's so important for us to finish strong. It's always exciting to see people encounter the Lord, whether the power of God fills them, they start weeping, they receive a breakthrough, or they just get really hungry for the Lord. But one thing that saddens me is when many of these young people go right back into their lifestyle, bondage, and addictions. It's sad because God does not want us to leave our encounters where we had them—at a conference, a church service, an altar call, or wherever. He wants us to continue in Him, from glory to glory.

Do you know people who began their walk with Jesus strong, but all of a sudden they lost their passion? Maybe you feel like you're that person. You were once burning for God, but life just got busy and you lost the reverence you once had, you lost the fire for the Word and for the secret place. This generation needs to see a fire that keeps burning. They will turn and glean from a fire that continues to burn through every season. The fire of God is not a seasonal fire. I believe Jesus wants to refresh you.

> *"Do you not know that in a race all the runners run, but only one receives the prize? So run that you may obtain it. [25] Every athlete exercises self-control in all things. They do it to get a crown that will not last, but we do it to get a crown that will last forever. [26] So I do not run aimlessly; I do not box as one beating the air. [27] But I discipline my body and keep it under control, lest after preaching to others I myself should be disqualified."*
> —1 Corinthians 9:24–27

The Apostle Paul said that we're running a race, and at the end of this race, there is a prize. Notice that his focus was on the end of the race. I remember a well-known evangelist would often encourage preachers, "Keep in mind the end from the beginning." When you start a sermon, you've always got to have the end in mind, knowing where you are taking people. When I'm on a car journey, I first want to make sure I have gas in the tank, none of my lights are broken, and my tires are properly inflated so that I can make it to my destination.

We see so many churches, ministries, and movements starting these days. Many of them start strong but toward the end, they lose their fire. We need to be those who don't just start strong but finish stronger! We're running a race, and we're not just going to get to the finish line, we're going to run for the prize because not everyone gets the prize.

When I was young, I loved to run. I would often run to a middle school about two miles from my house. One time I decided not to put any shoes on—I don't know what I was thinking—and thought, Maybe I'll run a little faster! So I took my shoes off and I ran those two miles, but on the way back my feet were a little bit tired and I clipped my foot against the concrete. I looked down and saw I had cut my toe open, and it started bleeding. I obviously had to stop running because of this interference—because I didn't keep in mind the end from the beginning!

There are two races that you can run. The first is for yourself. You can run a race for yourself, not knowing where you're headed. You may have some goals and desires, but there is no true end in sight. The second race is the one that God has perfectly marked out for you.

Sometimes as you're running the race you look beside you and behind you to see where everyone else is. And when you see someone getting close to you, you want to cut them off to make sure that you win the race. Remember the story of the turtle and the rabbit? The rabbit got distracted by what the turtle was doing and let its guard down. By the time the rabbit woke up, the turtle was already at the finish line!

When you're running the race, don't compare yourself to anybody else. Comparison is a killer of destiny. We each have a specific plan from God, and the enemy wants us to compare ourselves to other people, which can cause us to forfeit our race. The worst thing you can do is try to be somebody else. Every single body part, every single member in the house of God has a specific duty that God has placed there for them to accomplish. You have gifts in your life that nobody else has. I pray that your business, small group, church, or ministry does not compare itself to any other movement, evangelistic ministry, or prophetic ministry but that you only compare yourself to God's perfect will for you.

The problem today is that many people want an easy fix, a quick "how-to." They get the five points and create replicas. God is a creator, not just a replicator. He loves to create. That is why everyone is so different. Our differences complement each other and fulfill a bigger purpose. Unfortunately, so many ministries look the same that when someone actually hears from God, it's not normal and people do not like it. Why? People are uncomfortable with something different.

But those who hear from God and are close to Him have grace on them, an anointing and acceleration that people are not used to. When you meet those who are truly of the Spirit, you never know how they will go—they are like the wind.

People get so comfortable with their own ways that they think they don't have to go to God to hear Him. But doing what everyone is doing does not bring transformation to a generation. You cannot change a generation—only God can. God will use what you give Him, but He will do more with what He gives you. Allow Him to do it through you, His way!

> ***God will use what you give Him, but He will do more with what He gives you.***

I love looking at the end of people's lives or sitting with older people and asking them for wisdom, because it's at the end of a person's life that he or she begins to see things for what they are and realize what was important and what was not. The young people have the fire, zeal, and passion, but often the older people have the wisdom.

In Paul's final words to Timothy as he neared the end of his life, he said:

> *"I have fought the good fight, I have finished the race, I have kept the faith. 8 Henceforth there is laid up for me the crown of righteousness, which the Lord, the righteous judge, will award to me on that day, and not only to me but also to all who have loved his appearing."*
> —2 Timothy 4:7–8

In the beginning, Paul wrote to the Corinthians basically saying, "Run this race so that you can finish it and get the prize." Paul even cut Mark out of his ministry because he said Mark was unreliable, and this caused tension with Barnabas. But Paul's goal was to finish first, and anyone in his way needed to be removed.

At the end of his ministry, however, Paul said there was a crown laid up for him—not only for himself, but for "all who have loved his appearing" (v. 8). Toward the end of his life, Paul realized he was not the only one running this race, nor was he the only one getting the prize. He even came to the point when he asked to have Mark back because he was useful for the ministry.

Before, Mark had been in the way, but now Paul realized it wasn't only about him—there is not only one prize. The prize is actually for other people too. I believe that prize for me is other people we take with us to heaven. There will be no greater joy than seeing Jesus and seeing other people you brought to heaven with you. This is the heart of the Father and will become your heart as you find joy in Him.

When you're running your race, sometimes you will be able to grab somebody else and make sure they finish with you. When you see somebody fallen over or bleeding, you can help them up and encourage them to continue their race to the end. Don't compare yourself to others, but look for how you can bless somebody and uplift them. We're called to raise other people up and disciple them, just like Paul did for Timothy—not to make converts but disciples. God will truly reward you for this.

One reason people don't finish well is that they start to apply the principles of the world rather than the principles of the kingdom of God. They run their race so that they are first, but they always end up last. The first will be last, but the last will always be first.

The goal of the enemy is to bring the world into the church and mix things up so the church looks nothing like it's supposed to. "Do not be conformed to this world, but be transformed by the renewal of your mind" (Rom. 12:2). If the world looks at the church and sees no difference, they're not going to be attracted to our light. The enemy wants to throw us off from the main race and get our focus on worldly ways and worldly things when God has given this life for so much more.

I'm going to give you a key to finishing this race stronger than you started. The way to finish this race and come out on top, with joy, is to stay abiding in the presence of God. When you're running the race and you're equipped with the water of His presence, you will be able to persevere to the end. It's like putting on one of those backpacks with a tube so that you can drink water. You don't even need to stop to get a drink; you can just keep on running and drinking.

We need to get plugged back in and start drinking once again. We need to open the Word. We need to seek the Lord. We need to get on our knees and pray and fast, and not give up or slow down for anything! The enemy will always offer shortcuts to take you away from this place. Do not give in. Discern all things by the Spirit through prayer.

Jesus wants to equip you with everything you need to finish well. He wants to get your gaze back on Him, and not on your career, family, business, ministry, problems, or even the church. I pray that this book puts a spark in you, that a stirring begins in your heart and never stops from this moment forward, in Jesus' name. If you make the Lord your priority, He will take care of all the other things.

I declare that you will finish strong. You will see a generation on fire for Jesus Himself. The time to find joy in your prayer life is now. Close this book and pick up His book. Go into the secret place and seek Him. I pray that you remain in Him—He is your true joy.

ABOUT THE AUTHOR

MARK MOROZOV is the Founding Director of Global Revival. His heart's desire is to see a generation revived by Jesus, walking in its full potential in Jesus Christ. He longs to see many people impact their own spheres of influence. Mark is a worldwide traveling Revivalist preaching Jesus Christ with powerful signs and wonders following.

VISION STATEMENT

Revive the Body, Make Disciples, Awaken the Nations Through the Gospel

Our vision is to Awaken the Body of Christ from spiritual slumber, Ignite a passion for God's Kingdom, and Reform the Church to its original purpose. We believe that by Reviving the Body of Christ, we can transform the world and bring lasting change to every nation. We seek to unite believers from all walks of life, empower leaders, and equip the Church to become agents of transformation in their communities. Through prayer, worship, discipleship, and evangelism, we will awaken the nations to the reality of God's love and power, ignite a global movement of revival, and reform the Church to be a shining light in a dark world.

ABOUT THE MINISTRY

Global Revival was founded by Evangelist Mark Morozov in 2019. Our heart cry is to ignite the hearts of the saints to see souls saved, not just locally but also globally. We want to become a platform for the next generation. We will see the Great Commission fulfilled in partnership with many evangelists. The ministry focuses on different angles to equip the global body in evangelism and see the lost saved for Jesus Christ.

My friend, if the body of Christ needs anything, it is to be revived and equipped to go out and save other souls. Evangelism is like an essential vitamin to the Christian. At the end of our lives, we will stand before God. We can only bring ourselves and others, not any possessions or belongings. Because of this, we sponsor and send out young evangelists. We travel locally and globally to see God move in signs and wonders!

You can join us today in spreading the Gospel of Jesus Christ prayerfully and/or financially. Reach out to us on our website to connect with the team.

globalrevivalnow.com

Partner with us

HELP US BRING REVIVAL TO THE NATIONS BY PARTNERING WITH US MONTHLY

Socially

Global Revival is established on Social Media through various platforms. We would love for you to follow along with us as we seek to provide life-changing content. We believe that it is life-changing because our content here is to provoke you to fall more in love with him who is life, Jesus. You can subscribe, like, and follow along with us socially through: Youtube, Instagram, Tiktok, and Facebook.

Prayerfully

Prayer is a vital lifeline to what God has called us to do. We cannot do what we do without the faithful partnership of people around the world that are joining with us in prayer, intercession, and celebration of all that God is speaking and doing in the nations of the world.

Financially

Financial provision is very vital and is strategic part of the way God accomplishes the desires of His heart. It would be a great joy for our team and the advancing of what God has called us to do around the world if you would pray about partnering with us financially. There is a mutual blessing when we commit to what God is asking of us. We will share the reward for all that God is able to accomplish when we join together in partnership.

Visit our website:
www.globalrevivalnow.com/partner/

SELLING OUT EVERYWHERE WE ARE GOING

Author's Write-Up

There are many things we may find joy in, however, one thing that we do not associate with joy is suffering in life. There is much joy to be found through the sufferings we experience in life. Many times we thank God for blessings, but we do not thank Him for the suffering. Why should we thank Him for the hardships? Because He is with us in the midst of them. It is better to be with Jesus during the hardships than to be without him during the blessings. My hope is that this book will help direct your focus to Him instead of your own sufferings.

GET YOUR COPY TODAY

www.ingramcontent.com/pod-product-compliance
Lightning Source LLC
Chambersburg PA
CBHW071119160426
43196CB00013B/2637